bend-the-rules
SEWING

the essential guide to a whole new way to sew

amy karol

photography by
alexandra grablewski

POTTER
CRAFT

New York

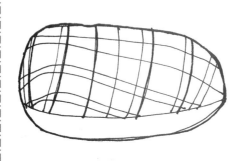

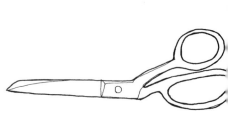

Published in the United States by Potter Craft,
an imprint of the Crown Publishing Group,
a division of Random House, Inc., New York.
www.crownpublishing.com
www.pottercraft.com

POTTER CRAFT and CLARKSON N. POTTER are
trademarks, and POTTER and colophon are
registered trademarks of Random House, Inc.

Library of Congress Cataloging-in-Publication Data
Karol, Amy.
    Bend the rules sewing : the essential guide to a
whole new way to sew / Amy Karol. — 1st ed.
        p.   cm.
ISBN: 978-0-307-34721-3
1. Machine sewing.   I. Title.
TT713.K37   2007
646.2—dc22   2006028126

ISBN 978-0-307-34721-3

Printed in China

Design by Lauren Monchik
Photography by Alexandra Grablewski
Illustrations by Amy Karol

10 9 8 7 6 5 4

First Edition

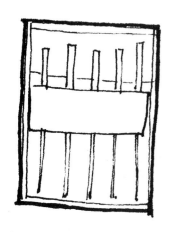

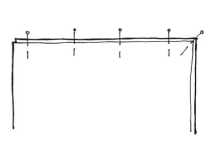

For Mom
and
Grandma,
my sewing heroes

contents

introduction

I love making stuff.

And I love sewing. And I sew a lot—a whole heck of a lot. From handbags, pillows, curtains, and clothes to small framed art quilts, modern abstract wall hangings, fabric paintings, and soft sculpture, I have sewn it all. I started my fabric and sewing obsession when I was just a wee one; I earned the title of "craft queen" at the tender age of four from my mother, a sewing junkie in her own right.

My house is filled with fabric. I wish I could tell you it is all folded neatly and color coordinated on shelves. Maybe someday it will be, but for now, when I need that special fabric, I dump out a bag (a huge garbage bag) and sit in the middle of the pile on the floor and look through it. I am literally sitting in huge piles of fabric several times a day. This horrifies my more organized sewing buddies. It's a sickness, I tell you, but a good one. I also love sharing my craft obsession with others. You want to learn how to sew? I can help you.

How many times have you been in a clothing or housewares shop and said, "I know I could make that if I knew how to sew." Well, you know what? You can. If you know how to sew, you can make that pillow you want in just the right shade of blue and actually hem the pants you never wear because they have always been a little too long. Sewing can be therapeutic. Like so many crafts, it's a way to keep your hands busy, feel good about making something yourself, and have fun—which is really the most important thing. When you know how to sew, you start thinking about shopping differently. Whipping together a homemade gift is easy and fun and so much better than going to the mall.

Sewing is easy and fast. With a sewing machine, some fabric, and some basic tools, you can make most of these projects in a few hours. This is more than just a sewing project book: I want you to love sewing as much as I do, so I write a lot about how to learn to sew with the least amount of frustration. I'll dispel some sewing myths and help you banish your perfectionism by explaining when to cut corners and when to take your time. Next, I will help you with basic sewing equipment needs and offer advice on buying machines, scissors, pins, patterns, and everything in between. Selecting the right fabric can make all the difference in a project. I'll also help you learn how to choose and what to avoid and why. Then I cover "The Basics." All the basic techniques needed to complete the projects in the book are here: basic fabric layout and cutting, stitches, hems, buttonholes, zippers, trims, bias binding, hand-embroidery stitches, and a lot more. It's all in one section.

This is a book for beginners, but it will also appeal to all levels of sewers. Some of the simple projects—like the pillows—offer variations with techniques that are more challenging and complex, teaching new skills to experienced sewers.

Almost all of the projects are fast, as in start-on-a-Saturday-and-finish-on-a-Sunday fast. They require neither a huge time commitment nor a lot of fabric. Quick projects plus not much money equals a very happy crafter, indeed.

I also teach tips for embellishing your fabric to make it your own. Many of the projects shown in this book are unusual because of something I have done to the fabric itself. For you artsy crafters who crave a one-of-a-kind look, these techniques teach you how to stamp, paint, and embroider your fabric.

So turn on your machine and get ready to learn how to sew in a new way.

—Amy Karol, 2007

Visit me online! I'd love to hear from you.
www.amykarol.com

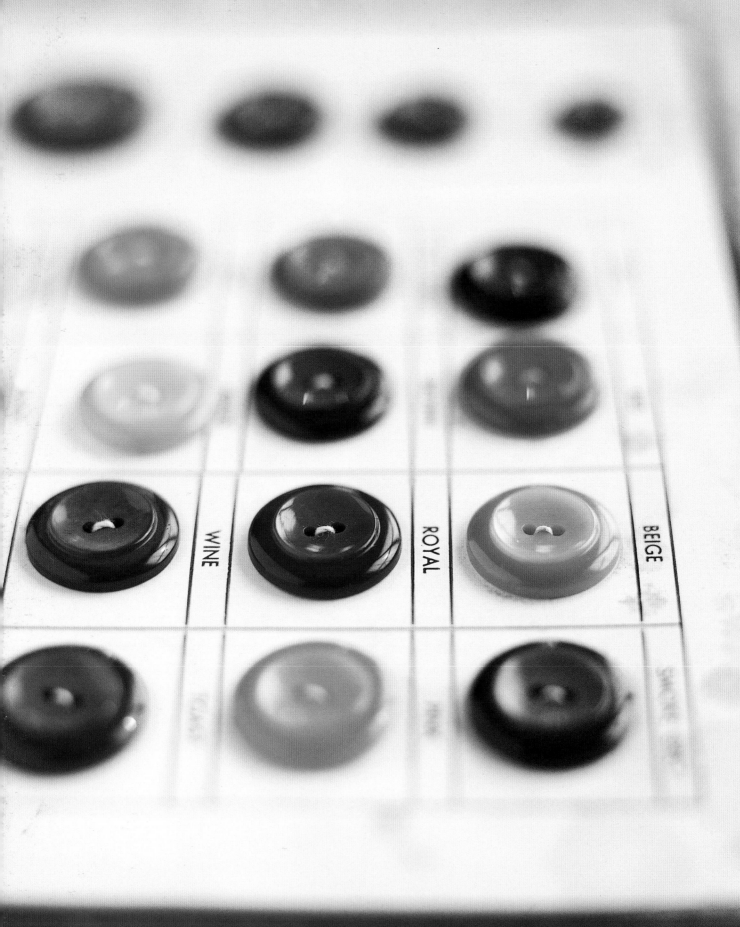

part 1 what you need to know

learning to sew 101

Bending the rules in sewing

Beginning sewers have a real advantage over those who have been doing it a long time.

I call it the "why not?" factor. New sewers tend to think differently than seasoned seamstresses. They don't know when they are breaking the rules, so they try crazy, adventurous things that can turn out fabulously. Breaking the rules can also be a catastrophe, but the adventurous idea is what is most important. The goal of this book is to help experienced sewers loosen up and teach new sewers some basic skills.

I like to bend the rules. Bend, but not break. My grandmother always used to tell my mom, "You have to be good enough to know when you can bend the rules." This has always stuck with me. Learning this approach will help you unleash your inner artist/ diva/fashion designer and keep the project from going haywire. The techniques in these projects give you a foundation. After you learn them, you can then use these skills on new projects you might design yourself, or even on existing clothes in your closet.

You don't have to sew everything from scratch. In fact, you don't even always have to "sew." Fabric markers, fabric paint, and rubber stamping are all wonderful ways to make a project look extra artsy.

I'll be bending the rules in the way I actually show you how to sew a project. I suggest some basic rules to ensure success, such as cutting out the fabric carefully and using an iron as you work, but I very seldom use pins, and for the most part, I suggest you don't, either. I also cover quick methods for applying bias trims and appliqué. None of these methods involves glue or fusible tape. They aren't shoddy, just quick.

At the end of most projects there are tips, hints, and suggestions for adding variations. I hate ruining a sewing project more than anything, so these tips are meant to help you avoid the OOPS!-factor in the project. This is the next best thing I can do after being there in the room with you while you work.

Bending the rules in life

Bending the rules is also an approach to crafting and being creative. It's a balance of following directions and doing your own thing. We all make rules for ourselves, even if we don't realize we do. Are the rules you have made for yourself holding you back? Creating should be fun. If your rules cause you stress, guilt, or any other negative emotion, take a step back and look at what is going on.

Being crafty is being creative, and creativity can be hard to handle sometimes. When you get in a rut and nothing is working out, or you feel uninspired, just relax and take a break. It's okay to have long periods of being "uncrafty." That's often when you can get the most inspiration, when you aren't looking for it.

Make it easy on yourself

If you have tried sewing before and been frustrated, you are not alone. If you have never tried sewing before and want to, but are intimidated, you are not alone. There are some real tricks, tools, and ways of thinking that can help.

Learning how to follow directions from beginning to end, even if you make mistakes, will teach you much more than making it up yourself. Sewing is such an old craft—almost everything has been done before. There is no reason to reinvent the wheel here. By just following a few patterns and learning a few basic skills, you can design your own projects, fine-tune your favorite methods, and throw caution to the wind. Just make a few projects first.

LET'S BANISH A FEW SEWING MYTHS

Sewing is hard.
No. Not if you read directions and cut carefully. It's very similar to knitting in that way. In knitting, you have to count and measure, and if you don't, you get crazy results. The same is true in sewing: If you start well, it will end well.

Sewing machines are expensive.
Well, they can be, but used ones are not, and there are wonderful options. Machines that don't have an LCD or computer component are especially affordable. They tend to be cheaper to work on and can last longer. Each year I see more and more inexpensive machines come out that are geared for the beginning sewer, and these work just fine. If you love sewing, you may want a better machine that has more options, but if you have no machine at all, an inexpensive beginning machine is a great option.

Sewing takes a long time.
It can, but usually it doesn't. Even if you were to be a pessimist and factor in all the mistakes you might make, such as taking out stitches, sewing still takes a fraction of the time of many other crafts. And that sounds pretty good to me. Sewing is fast, but it's not portable. To make a project quickly, it's best to have a dedicated sewing area. It doesn't have to be a craft room, just a place where you can sit down to your machine.

If I sew something, it will look homemade.
And that's a good thing! Actually, it won't look homemade, but it will look unique, which will cause people to ask, "Oh, did you make that?" Because people are so used to seeing things mass-produced, something handmade really does stand out. The next question they will ask is, "Can you make me one?" or "Do you sell those?" And I will leave those answers up to you.

What to do when you need the seam ripper: Your attitude about mistakes

When you make a mistake, like sewing a bad seam, what do you do? It's best to try to fix something the moment it happens. Get some coffee or turn on some music and slowly rip out the seam.

Sometimes it's not that simple. Maybe it started at the beginning. Was it cut out wrong? Too short? Maybe there were uneven seam allowances? Can you actually salvage it without scrapping the whole thing? And if you can't, can you live with it as is, imperfections and all?

I say give it a few days (or at least a few hours). Look at it then. Usually it's okay, and not as bad as you had thought. Mistakes are always much less noticeable in a week or so, and in a month, the project will look amazing.

Having said that, sometimes it might be a good idea to start over. If you have to remake a project, it will always go faster the second time around, because you will already know what to do differently. Also, sometimes a project is just jinxed. There's really no other way to put it, it just is. Better to start fresh and leave that bad juju behind.

Ultimately, it's your call, but remember that mistakes are good. You may want to punch me for saying this, because it sounds so annoying, but really, you can learn a ton from making mistakes. The key is to take the time to avoid making the same ones over and over. When you do make a mistake, try to laugh about it, cut yourself some slack, and eat a cupcake.

LET'S BANISH A FEW SEWING MYTHS continued

Sewing can save you a ton of money. I hear myself saying, "Buy a sewing machine, it will pay for itself!" all the time, and for the most part, that is true. However, there are a few things to keep in mind. Labor in this world is cheap. Nowadays you can get almost anything you want at a large discount store for less money than making it from scratch. If your main goal for a particular project is to be creative and have fun, you will be happy. If your main goal is to save money, do some homework first, check fabric prices, and take the time to figure out costs.

let's get started!

Sew it up: The sewing machine

If you are a new sewer, try to borrow a machine from someone before buying. Older machines last a long time, so ask around. Chances are you can find one among your family or friends. If you do borrow a machine, make sure it works. It should sew a straight line without getting tangles in the bobbin or anything else equally frustrating. A basic machine is all you need for the projects in *Bend-the-Rules Sewing*. A buttonhole stitch is nice, and it is standard on most machines. A darning foot option (for free-motion quilting) also is standard on most machines or available as a separate foot attachment.

If your old sewing machine needs to be serviced, the price can vary greatly depending on what's out of whack. The service shop may suggest replacing the old one with a new machine, especially if they happen to sell sewing machines. Be careful, though. Unless you are buying a really good new machine, or if repairing the old machine is too expensive, it's probably best to just get the old machine repaired.

Buying a sewing machine: The lowdown

A good sewing machine can easily last twenty to thirty years or longer. I am using the same machine I got when I was eighteen. I'm now thirty-four, and I don't plan to replace it anytime soon. It was a good, solid machine when I bought it, not top of the line, but not the low-end model, either. I think good tools make all the difference. If I were buying a sewing machine, I'd buy the best one I could afford. And if you need a bit of help rationalizing a good machine, then consider this: it will pay for itself in no time with all the gifts you can make.

Where do you buy new sewing machines?

You can buy a new machine in lots of places, from discount department stores to sewing machine stores (often, they also sell vacuum cleaners, which I love). If you get an inexpensive machine at a discount store you probably won't be able to try it first unless they have a demo model. For what you are paying, that's okay. Look for the following basics:

a straight stitch, reverse stitch, zigzag stitch, buttonhole stitch, and a zipper foot. These less-expensive machines tend not to sew well on sheer or heavyweight fabrics, like denim, and they are not built to stand up to really heavyweight projects, like upholstery.

I recommend buying from a sewing machine store. These stores allow you to sit at the sewing machines and really try them out before buying. Machines sold at these stores tend to be more expensive but are the best brands. The sales people will help you determine which machine is the best for you. These shops often offer confidence-building free classes and sometimes even clubs. The best have their own service departments, too. Sewing shops also usually allow trade-ins, which is something to consider. If you buy a low-end model and in a few years want to upgrade, the shop will usually take the old model as a trade-in. Ask about this when you are deciding what to buy.

If you want to try machine-quilting by "drawing" with the thread, find a machine that allows you to drop the feed dogs and free-motion quilt, also referred to as a darning stitch. Even if you don't understand what this is right now, you want it. The top-of-the-line machines also embroider, which is a whole other world of decorative sewing and often involves a computer and software and all kind of things I won't go into here. These machines can be astoundingly expensive, so knowing the type of sewing you think you will do is important in choosing the right machine.

How to make friends with your machine

Now that you have a machine (whether new, borrowed, or used), get to know it. Plan an hour or two to sit down and read the manual. Learn to thread your machine. Make a cheat sheet if it helps you, and post it near your machine. Keep the manual handy, too.

If you have an old machine, the manual might be missing. If so, look online, as there are sites devoted to helping replace old manuals. If it's portable, take your machine to a sewing machine shop and see if you can order a new manual that would work with your old model. Ask the shop's service department folks to show you how to thread the machine and wind thread onto the bobbin.

SUPPLIES CHECKLIST

Cut it up: Scissors and other things
Bent-handle dressmaker's shears
Sewing scissors
Seam ripper
Rotary cutter (optional)
Self-healing mat (optional)

Measure it: Embrace accuracy
Tape measure
Big clear plastic ruler (optional)
Small ruler

Mark it up: Markers and chalk
Fabric marking pens (water soluble)
Fabric paint (optional)
Fabric rubber-stamp pads (optional)
Fabric markers/decorative (optional)
Marking chalk
Adhesive and/or narrow masking tape
Freezer paper

Flatten it: Get to know your iron
Iron
Iron cleaner
Ironing board and pad
Pressing cloth
Pressing ham (optional)
Mini iron (optional)

Stick it: Pins and needles
Sewing machine needles
Hand-sewing needles
Pins
Pincushion

Other notions
Thimbles
Sewing machine thread
Hand-sewing thread
Beeswax
Bodkin (optional)
Bias tape makers

Basic sewing tools and notions

Here's a list of supplies you'll need to make the projects in this book. When you sew clothing, you'll need a few more things, but since we are doing very little of that in this book, we'll save that list for another time. Some items are marked optional. Keep in mind, however, that the right tools make these projects easier to sew.

Cut it up: Scissors and other things

Bent-handle dressmaker's shears

Use this pair to cut fabric. They should have 8" (20.5cm) blades and a 45-degree bend at the pivot point. All-metal Gingher scissors are my best friends, but some sewers prefer scissors with plastic handles because they are much lighter. Use these scissors on fabric only—never for other crafts, especially paper. My mom threatened us repeatedly when we were little about using her sewing scissors, and now I can see why. A good pair can easily last a few lifetimes. Buy the best, guard them well, and get them sharpened every few years. **A**

Sewing scissors

Smaller than your fabric shears with straight, 6" (15cm) or less blades, this pair lives by your machine and is used for clipping all the tiny threads. If they are on sale, buy two pairs of this size. You will use these for hand-sewing projects as well. **B**

Seam ripper

With luck, you won't need it often, but when you need to take out stitches, this little fellow will ease the pain. **C**

Rotary cutter (optional)

If you think you will be making a lot of quilts, it's worth getting one of these. It is a metal circle on a handle, and, when used with a plastic straightedge on a cutting mat, it allows you to cut straight fabric pieces quickly and accurately. You can also buy rotary-blade sharpeners, which are less expensive in the long run, because replacement blades for this cutter aren't cheap. **D**

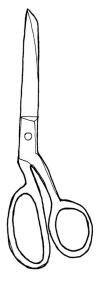

A Bent-handle dressmaker's shears

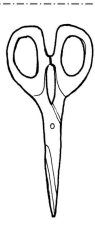

B Sewing Scissors

C Seam ripper

Basic sewing tools and notions

Self-healing mat (optional)
This is used with the rotary cutter; see page 19.

Measure it: Embrace accuracy

Tape measure
These used to be made of fabric, but now are made of vinyl.
Buy two, because they are inexpensive and disappear fast,
especially if you have children. I always wear one around my
neck when I sew. **E**

Big clear plastic ruler (optional)
A 6" (15cm) by 24" (61cm) one is often used as a straightedge
for the rotary cutter; see page 19.

Small ruler
Keep this next to your machine for handy reference. A 6"
(15cm) to 8" (20.5cm) length is fine.

Mark it up: Markers and chalk

Fabric marking pens (water soluble)
These aren't decorative; they are used to mark guidelines and
trace pattern outlines or templates onto fabric. The lines will
disappear in cold water, but they can become permanent if
they come in contact with heat, so remove marks before you
iron. These work best on light-colored cottons. To remove the
lines, use a spray bottle filled with cold water. **F**

Fabric paint (optional)
This is special paint used for fabric that can be heat set, allow-
ing you to wash and dry the item without having the paint
wash away.

Fabric rubber-stamp pads (optional)
These are for stamping patterns onto fabric; most of them
require heat setting.

Fabric markers/decorative (optional)
These are for drawing permanent designs directly onto your
fabric. Most types of these pens don't need to be heat set, but

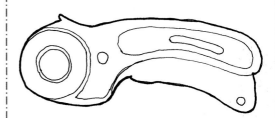

D Rotary cutter

E Tape measure

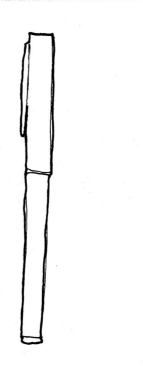

F Fabric marking pen

experiment before use and do lots of tests. Different colors act differently on the fabric. These are better for line art than for coloring shapes.

Marking chalk
For this book's projects, look for chalk pencils or triangles. They work well on wools and dark fabrics, and they wash off with water. **G**

Adhesive and/or narrow masking tape
Use tape as a handy way to mark top-stitching lines between two seams. It peels right off when you are done sewing, but remove it promptly so the sticky part doesn't bond to the fiber.

Freezer paper
This is an old-school type of kitchen paper, not waxed paper. It's made by Reynolds and others. It has one coated side and one plain side. Iron this onto your fabric to stabilize it for transferring templates and for painting and marking. It's also used for appliqué work.

Flatten it: Get to know your iron

Iron
Your iron is your best friend when you sew. Get a good model, one that has an on/off steam function. Don't use it on messy crafts projects, because the gunk will come off onto your fabric and glue will fuse to your iron.

Iron cleaner
Despite the advice above, I know you probably won't buy a dedicated sewing iron and will use your iron for both sewing and gunky crafts projects. So invest in a good iron plate cleaner—just in case. **H**

Ironing board and pad
Make sure your ironing board pad is thick. Pads sold with ironing boards often are not, and serious power-pressing can emboss the board's metal grill pattern on your fabric. Cut up an old towel or an old flannel sheet and slip it under the ironing pad for extra padding.

G Marking chalk

H Iron cleaner

The iron is your best friend when you sew.

Basic sewing tools and notions

Pressing cloth

These are not really necessary on cottons, but some fabrics, like linen, silk, and corduroy, will get shiny if you iron on them directly. Iron on the wrong side or use a cloth to protect the fabric on the front. A pressing cloth can be muslin, cotton, or flannel—just a big scrap of natural fiber. An old cut up pillow-case would work well.

Pressing ham (optional)

These projects don't require one, but it's nice to have and really necessary if you sew clothes. Plus, it is just a fun thing to have around because it's called a ham. Garment-makers use this to press onto when shaping a curve. I

Mini iron (optional)

Mini irons are handy for making small shapes when doing appliqué work. I love mine, but I didn't have one for years and survived just fine. If you like to work small, you should try one. They are very nice to have. Be careful, though, there is a high burn potential with these little fellows. J

Stick it: Pins and needles

Sewing machine needles

Check your machine manual for a recommended brand. The needle size and type is determined by your fabric, but when in doubt, "universal size 12" is a safe bet. For heavier weights—wools and corduroy—go to a higher number. For fine fabrics—thin linens and silks—go to a lower number. There are special needles for stretchy fabrics and denim. Keep them in the packaging they are sold in so you don't use the wrong one. K

Hand-sewing needles

Use these for embellishments and sewing on things like buttons and bindings. Sharps are good all-purpose needles. They have round eyes and sharp points. Chenille needles are great for decoration. They have a larger eye and can be used with thicker thread.

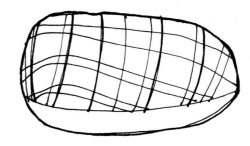

I Pressing ham

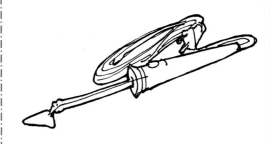

J Mini iron

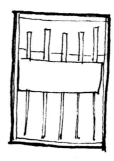

K Sewing machine needles

Basic sewing tools and notions

Hand-sewing tip: Your needle should be thicker than the thread you are using. If it's not, it won't make a large enough hole and you will really have to tug to pull the thread through the fabric.

Pins
These are what you use to keep the fabric together while you sew. I like pins with ball heads the best, and unless you are using really delicate fabrics, they are good for just about everything.

Pincushion
Every sewer deserves the ubiquitous tomato pincushion, so that should be the first one on your list. The modern sewer could also get the magnetic kind, which is handy to hold pins in large quantities; they stick to the magnet, which makes picking up spilled pins really easy. Pincushions are simple to make, and you will want several. Plan to have at least two. Keep one by your machine—so you have a place to put the pins when you take them out as you sew— and one where you cut out your fabric so you can pin the pattern pieces on. **L**

Other notions

Thimbles
These are for hand sewing when using a sharp needle. You will get a tender finger if you do much hand sewing, and a thimble will help. Some sewers just can't use thimbles, so we get a callus instead. Either way, most thimbles are cheap and come in many styles and sizes and in metal, leather, and even plastic, so try some until you find one that works for you. **M**

Sewing machine thread
I use polyester thread in my machine for most sewing projects, and that's what I recommend for beginning sewers.

I match the color to the main fabric I am working with in a slightly lighter shade. It will show up less. Avoid buying really cheap thread. You want your quilts and crafts to last a long time. Fabric shops can help you here. Find a salesperson,

L Pincushion

M Thimbles

tell her what you are making, and get help selecting the best thread. There are many kinds, and the print is small on these spools of thread. I can't tell you how many times I have picked up something completely inappropriate without realizing it. Once you get help, you will become familiar with where the different types of thread are displayed. N

Hand-sewing thread
For decorative work, six-strand embroidery floss or twisted pearl cotton is great. Embroidery floss can be separated into fewer strands; the pearl cotton you use as is.

Beeswax
Run the thread though this to keep it from fraying and getting tangled. This is one of those things that will make you wonder how you lived without it. O

Bodkin (optional)
Use this for pulling cord or fabric though a casing, or turning a tube inside out. It's a necessity when you want to use a drawstring or elastic waistband. P

Bias tape makers
I love binding. If you want to make your own, using any fabric you want, you will need this tool. It is a flattened metal cone that you feed your fabric strip into. As you pull the fabric through and iron, folded fabric trim comes out the other end. These come in different widths, and I use them all the time. I love them a heck of a lot. Very clear, easy-to-follow directions are included with these tools. Q

N Sewing machine thread

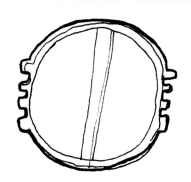

O Beeswax

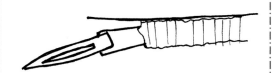

P Bodkin

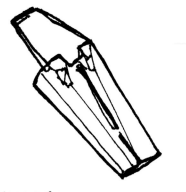

Q Bias tape maker

Your sewing area (and how to make it fit in your life)

Convenience is key. Let's say you want to sew something simple, like a coaster. Let's then say that in order to sew that coaster you have to lug your machine out from under the bed, drag the iron from the laundry room, and unfold a card table (or take over the dining table), all for five minutes of work. Chances are you will buy coasters instead.

A desk in a spare room, a table in the corner of a living room, or even a bedroom is fine if you don't have a dedicated craft room. You can throw a lovely bit of fabric over your machine (or sew yourself a sewing machine cozy!) when you aren't using it to keep off dust. Store your projects in a plastic bin tucked under the table.

If you don't have a dedicated space, the ironing will need some planning. If you think you are going to make mostly small projects, a tabletop ironing board is great. Then you iron on the table right next to your machine. I prefer a full-sized ironing board, and you can hang one on the wall nearby and just set it up every time you sew. It's an extra step, but it doesn't take long. I always have my ironing board at a right angle to my table, and set at the same height as, or slightly lower than, my tabletop. With the pivot of my chair to the right, I can iron very quickly, without having to stand up and sit down again.

There are a lot of accessories out there to organize your notions. I love using a vintage sewing basket. Do what makes sense to you. You don't need to spend a lot of money. Large Ziploc bags are a great way to store buttons, trims, zippers, and tapes, especially if you are just going to keep them in drawers. I do recommend a wood rack for your sewing machine thread up near your machine, but even that isn't necessary.

Two things I think are really important are lots of light and physical comfort. You will be concentrating while you sew and may not be aware of compromising your posture or your eyesight until you are already fatigued. Make sure that you have a good chair and that your setup is right for your back or wrists. Get a good task lamp and increase your light if you are getting headaches and straining your eyes.

Fabric

Storing fabric

Fabric is best kept folded on shelves so it can breathe. To minimize dust, some sewers use plastic bins. I keep mine all throughout the house in garbage bags. I don't recommend this system and hope one day to remedy it. If you have yardage you will be keeping for a long time, the best way to store it is to roll it on a large tube. This is especially kind on silks or other special fabric that will show creases easily.

How to buy fabric

For these projects, I use either vintage fabrics or almost exclusively 100 percent cotton quilting fabric. Cotton quilting fabric comes in so many wonderful patterns—it's by far my favorite. The typical width is 45" (114cm), folded on a 22" (56cm) bolt. The long tubes of fabric you see are usually 60" (152cm) wide. These are often found in the home décor section, tend to be more expensive, and are sometimes thicker, but check them out and don't limit yourself. Just pay attention to how a fabric feels and imagine your project being made of it. If it seems suitable, it probably is. When you sew clothing, you need to be more selective with your fabric selections, but for these projects, not so much.

The fabric bolt label

Look here to get all the info you need about a fabric. It's all printed on the top edge of the bolt or sometimes hidden under the fabric. The manufacturer and pattern name, the content and shrinkage, and the width and price will all be here. If any of this is not clear, ask for help. The most common widths are 45" (114cm) or 54" (137cm). If you are using cotton quilting fabric, you will mostly see 45"- (114cm-) wide fabric. This can be deceiving because it's folded in half and then rolled on the bolt, so when you get it cut, you will only see half the width.

If a fabric feels suitable, it probably is.

Yardage increments

A yard is 36" (91cm). So when you take a bolt of fabric that's 45" (114cm) wide up to the counter and ask for a yard, you will get a 36" x 45" (91 x 114cm) piece; but it will be folded in half, so it will appear to be 36" x 22" (91 x 56cm). This is good to know when you are designing your own pillows and curtains. Most shops have a minimum of a ¼- or ⅛-yard cut. Online shops usually have a half-yard cut minimum. A half-yard is a generous piece of fabric for most projects, about a 18" x 45" (45 x 114cm) rectangle.

Two things can throw you a curve: the shrinkage after you prewash and the direction of the fabric pattern. The first issue is simple: buy a bit extra and expect your fabric to shrink. Buying a ¼ yard (.2m) more than you think you will need is easier than running short.

The second issue can be confusing. Let's say you are designing a drapery panel and you want the stripes to run vertical and you need each panel to be about 45" (114cm) wide. Simple. You just measure the length and off you go. But when you get to the fabric store, the stripes run the other way on the fabric. You can't just hang a 45"- (114cm-) wide piece of fabric. If you do, the stripes will run horizontal. So now you have to change your quantity, have some waste, and possibly add seams to get the panel long enough—not what you planned at all. Fortunately, stripes almost always run parallel to the selvage edge, but other directional patterns might not, so keep this in mind when selecting fabrics.

Fabric shop experience

Fabric shop owners and their salespeople like to sew and are there to help you. So ask away and tell them what you are making. The more information you can give them, the more they can help. When you are ready to have fabric cut, take the bolt to the counter. Here's your chance to lay it out and really see the fabric before it is cut. Don't rush this step. Tell the salesperson how much you need, ask to see how much that is (look for any flaws), and then have her cut it. There are normally no returns on cut fabric. And if you are in doubt, always get a ¼-yard (.2m) extra. Unless you have a huge stash of buttons, thread, and trims at home, it's best to buy everything you need to complete a project at once.

STABILITY IN YOUR LIFE: INTERFACING AND FACING

In many sewing projects, especially handbags, you need interfacing to give fabric stability. If you make a bag without it, you will get a droopy, empty, pillowcase-looking thing—very disappointing. The more shape and structure you want your bag to have, the more rigid the interfacing has to be. But I don't like most interfacings. They are usually synthetic and iron-on, which means you have to press them on the fabric, and they smell like glue and are stiff. Often, they don't stay adhered to the fabric, lifting over time, and then giving the surface of the bag a puckered look. Also, because interfacings are ironed on, the fabric doesn't behave like fabric anymore. The drape, movement, and hand change, and it just really gets on my nerves. (I admit these are highly personal pet peeves, and to many crafters, these really aren't a big deal.)

I have dealt with these problems in two ways. When I need a bag to have a rigid form, I use a superheavyweight interfacing in the bottom only. Or, I just use cotton flannel as the interfacing on all parts. I really love using cotton flannel because it is soft and adds weight and body but isn't too stiff. It is easily washable, unlike many iron-on interfacings. Cotton flannel works in the middle of place mats and handbags, and as the backing on a bib. I use a cotton flannel layer in just about everything. I buy large quantities of it in either off-white or white. Always wash and dry it first.

Experiment and see what *you* like. Some wonderful bags have been made using an iron-on polar fleece as an interfacing. This gives the bag a pleasing, soft feel, adds stability, and gives the piece a slightly puffy look, which works well for some bag styles. It is not cheap and can cost almost as much as the fabric, but it might also be a good material to experiment with.

TIPS AND TRICKS THAT WILL MAKE YOU A HAPPY SEWER

These helpful sewing habits are good to get into now, because they will simplify your life—at least in the sewing room. Bending the rules only works if you have some basic, solid sewing habits as a foundation.

Use a new sewing machine needle when you start a new project.

I am embarrassed that it took me so long to catch on to how important this is. Sewing machine needles work really hard, and changing needles can make your machine feel brand new. I have had needles in my machine for months at a time. My seams would start to look bunched and puckered, and I'd fiddle with the machine tension, thinking my machine needed to be serviced. When I changed my needle, the machine sewed through the fabric like a hot knife through butter. This is especially important when using lightweight fabrics or anything with a satin finish, because a dull needle will damage the surface of the fabric. Now I change my machine needle constantly, but if changing your needle after every project seems excessive, try changing it after every other project. This really makes a huge difference.

Trim as you go.

See all the little threads at the beginning and end of a seam? Get rid of them before you sew your next stitch. Trim them off every time you take that fabric away from the machine. Do this by cutting right up close to the edge of the fabric. If you don't, they can get caught up under the next bit of stitching. These threads are messy and annoying. Just say goodbye to them right away. Tape a little plastic baggie garbage sack to the edge of your sewing table really close to your hands so you can quickly throw them away.

Iron as you go.

The iron is your best friend when you sew. For these projects, seams can be either ironed to one side or pressed open. When you iron, pay attention to the right side of the fabric. Press seams really flat with no folds. From the front, you should almost be able to see the stitching where the two edges meet. Use steam, especially for cotton. You can fix a ton of little bumps and mistakes with a good pressing. I've been known to spend more time shaping and manipulating with the iron than sewing at the machine.

Have your iron next to your sewing machine.

This is a handy tip for speedy sewing. I set my ironing board up at a right angle to, and the same height as, my sewing table, so I just swivel in my chair to iron, and then swivel back to my machine. I never have to get up from my chair. Lazy? Heck, yeah!

Keep a small pair of sharp scissors next to your machine.

This is for cutting the little threads I was telling you about earlier. It's really nice to have a small, dedicated pair of scissors for this task.

Hang on to the thread tails when you start sewing.

Then they won't get pulled down into the machine (I call this the sewing undertow). Every time I get lazy and don't do this, I get tangles—and swearing ensues.

Practice sewing a straight line.

Here's a test: start a long piece of scrap fabric through your machine using a straight stitch and then stop using your hands. The fabric should feed through by itself, and the machine should sew a straight line. This means only a gentle hand is needed when holding your fabric. Pulling from the back will cause uneven stitches and is way more work for you. The machine will feed the fabric through; all your hands should be doing is lifting it up off the table and guiding it through corners and turns. If your hands are doing more than that, you are messing with the fabric too much. And if your machine doesn't behave in the way I just described, have it serviced.

When you start to sew, take a little backstitch at the beginning and end of your stitch.

This is so when you are monkeying around with it—ironing seams open and pinning—the ends won't start to come undone. Backstitches make ripping out the seams a bit harder, but you won't be doing that very often. We're thinking positive here.

Make your sewing machine work for you.

Your machine is supposed to help you, not hinder you. Most basic machines come with special feet to make tasks easier, such as a zipper foot, buttonhole foot, walking foot, and sometimes a foot for thick fabrics.

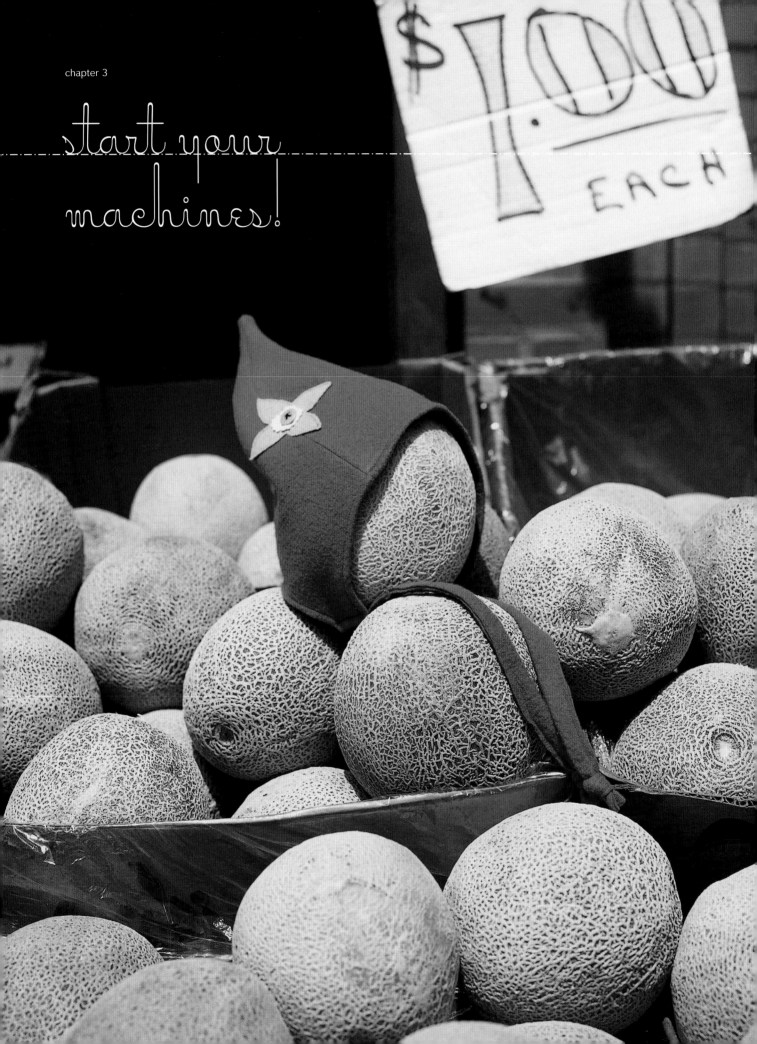

start your machines!

Sewing vocabulary 101

appliqué: Stitched by hand or machine, appliqué is a method of applying a piece of fabric, usually in a shape, on top of another piece of fabric.

basting: Stitching used to hold two pieces of fabric together before sewing with a more permanent stitch. Usually done close to the fabric edge and then removed later. If done by machine, it's the longest stitch setting. It's often used to make gathers by pulling one thread tight to draw up the fabric.

batting: In quilt-making, this material is the middle layer between the top and bottom of a quilt sandwich. This filling can be cotton, wool, or another soft material.

bias: Bias is the 45-degree angle that runs diagonally across the lengthwise grain of fabric. A piece of fabric "cut on the bias" drapes and can stretch. It's also used in narrow strips to make bias trim.

bias tapes: Fabric strips that come in different widths with pre-folded edges (also referred to as bias strips when making your own). They are perfect for finishing raw edges of fabric and can be bought premade in packages in different colors and widths. Make your own using fabric strips cut on the bias, which allows them to be used on curves.

binding: An edge-finishing treatment using bias tapes or straight-grain binding, binding is often folded double and covers the raw edges and batting of a quilt or other projects. The bias tape mentioned above is a type of binding.

fabric grain: This is the lengthwise or crosswise thread in a woven fabric. Look at your fabric closely and you will see threads running in two directions. This is the grain. If you make a tiny cut in most fabrics, you can tear the fabric "on the grain." It's important to lay out patterns on the grain correctly by matching the arrows on the pattern pieces.

fabric width: The measurement of the fabric from selvage edge to selvage edge is the width.

finger pressing: Using your finger to press a narrow edge of fabric over, often when appliquéing. Works well on small seams when an iron is too big.

hand: This refers to the way a fabric feels and drapes.

interfacing: A layer of interfacing fabric is either sewn into or ironed between the decorative fabrics to add structure and stability. Interfacing can be woven or non-woven. I use cotton flannel for most interfacing. I also use the term "facing" to mean the same thing.

lining: The lining fabric is on the "inside" of a project—the inside fabric of a handbag, for example. You see it, but only when you look inside.

miter: A type of corner treatment, a miter is a diagonal fold in the corner in an edge finish, such as a binding, and it's usually 45 degrees.

notions: A tool or accessory for sewing pins, zippers, thread, or anything used for a project that is not the fabric.

seam allowance: This is the measurement, usually expressed in fractions of inches in the United States, that extends outside the sewing line. For example, if a pattern has a ¼" (6mm) seam allowance included, then you cut out the pattern and sew your seams ¼" (6mm) in from the edge.

selvage: The finished edge of fabric, the selvage runs parallel to the lengthwise grain of fabric. If you buy fabric at a shop, yardage will have two selvage edges, which won't unravel and usually have the manufacturer's name printed on one edge.

stay stitching: Stay stitching is done inside the seam allowance, before construction, to stabilize curved or slanted edges. Usually done on a single thickness, but also used to attach interfacing. This is a normal straight seam in a normal length.

stitching in the ditch: This is top stitching on a project where two pieces are joined by a seam. Stitching in the ditch usually is done on a quilt through all layers.

Using the patterns in this book

Many of these projects use simple shapes, such as rectangles. The measurements of the rectangles you need will be given, but there is no pattern. Others call for patterns, which appear at the back of the book (the page number will be listed after the seam allowance). If the project includes a pattern, make a copy of the pattern at a copy shop and enlarge, if necessary. It's not a bad idea to cover the paper pattern copies with clear vinyl if you think you will be making a project more than once. Then pin the pattern to the fabric and cut around it carefully.

Several projects will have pattern pieces cut on a fold so both sides are symmetrical. You don't want to cut on the fold line; line it up with a folded edge of the fabric. If you accidentally cut along the fold line, you will need to cut out another piece. (Think paper snowflakes.)

Transferring a design template

I'm using the term "template" when there is a design that is not a pattern piece but is instead applied to the fabric, such as a hand-stitching design, a painting design, or machine quilting. I like to transfer template designs by using a window as a light box. Tape your paper copy of the template to a window. Then iron freezer paper to the wrong side of the fabric the design will be applied to. The freezer paper backing will keep the fabric from shifting. (See The Basics for ironing on freezer paper.) Now tape the freezer-backed fabric over the design on the window and use your water-soluble pen to trace the design on the top of your fabric.

Another method is to use dressmaker's tracing paper and a tracing wheel (a little wheel with teeth), which transfers marks to the fabric. This works best when you use it on the wrong side of the fabric because the marks don't always come off well. It's good to know about this method, but I don't recommend it for the projects in this book.

"RIGHT SIDES TOGETHER, TURN AND PRESS." (WHAT THE HECK DOES THIS MEAN?)

This phrase comes up in almost every project. It's one of those concepts that can be confusing if you think about it too much, so don't. Simply, it means that when you sew two pieces of fabric together, you always want the right sides of the fabric facing each other. Then, when you turn the piece right side out, the seams are on the inside.

This can get confusing when you are also sewing lining and facing pieces at the same time, but just remember that the outside fabrics should always be the ones facing each other.

When you turn something right side out, take your time; don't stretch and pull too hard. Ease the material through and then take the time to iron the piece into the right shape once it is turned. Ironing at this point is really important, so don't rush it and be extra careful on the corners of projects such as the coasters or place mats. Poking too hard from the inside to form the corners can stretch them and create an ear that will distort the shape of the rectangle. It's better to have the corner slightly rounded than distorted.

The Basics:
Handy sewing techniques to help you make your projects

How to pin

I don't use pins very much, but I do use them when sewing long seams or small curves. Insert pins about 6" (15cm) apart, perpendicular to the edge of the fabric. For small projects, pin much closer together, about every 2" (5cm), or more wherever there is a curve or corner. **A**

How to sew a seam

Check the seam allowance, which is usually ¼" (6mm) in these projects unless otherwise noted. Put fabric edges together and lift up the presser foot on your sewing machine. Insert fabric and lower foot. Take a few stitches, then back stitch, and then stitch forward again. Do not pull fabric through; it will feed itself. When you are at the end, backstitch again. If you have pins in the fabric, do not sew over them. You can break a needle this way, which is not only a drag but also really dangerous—stop when you come to a pin and take it out before you continue. **B**

To keep the seam allowance even, it helps to watch the edge of the fabric, not the needle. Use the markings on the throat plate of your machine to line up the edge of the fabric. For this method to work you need both fabric pieces to be even, so that's why cutting carefully is so important.

Ripping out a seam

With any luck, you won't have to do this often. Slide the tip of the seam ripper under the stitches on one side of the seam and gently cut through. This will take a bit more work at the beginning and end of the seam where you have backstitched. Do this every three to four stitches and then carefully pull the seam apart. Don't just take the ripper and cut down the middle of the seam—you could accidentally slice into the fabric. Make sure to remove all the loose threads and iron to reduce the size of the holes.

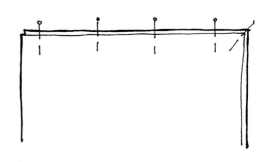

A

B

HOW MUCH FABRIC SHOULD I BUY? (OR, I LOVE THIS FABRIC AND HAVE TO BUY IT, BUT HAVE NO IDEA WHAT I'M GOING TO MAKE WITH IT)

With projects like these, you don't need much fabric, and you can be creative when you use it. For instance, if you only have enough of a great fabric for the outside of a handbag, use a different fabric for the lining. A good rule of thumb is to buy a half-yard if you like it a lot. If you love it more than anything in the world, buy one or two yards. I'd recommend more if we were talking about clothes, but since these projects are small, this should be plenty. You can use any scrap for all kinds of things: patches, doll clothes—you name it.

Sewing curves and corners

To sew a curve, adjust the fabric so that the edge is always even with the throat plate marking you are following on the machine. The goal here is to keep the fabric turning around the curve; don't straighten the fabric out and sew a straight line. If the corner is really tight, leave the needle in the fabric, raise the presser foot, and pivot the fabric a bit; then lower the presser foot and keep going. Go slowly and you will be fine.

For corners, stitch straight off the edge and then start again going in the perpendicular direction. This makes a much stronger corner than leaving the needle in and pivoting the fabric.

Top stitch

This a decorative straight stitch, typically sewn ¼" (6mm) from the edge of the fabric. It's done with the right side of the fabric facing up, through all layers. **C**

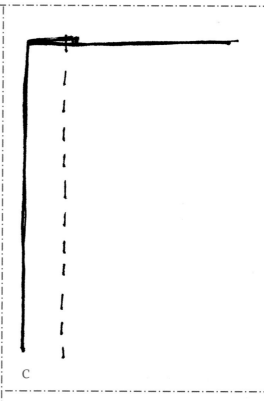

C

Edge stitch

Same as a top stitch, only narrower, about ⅛" (3mm) away from the fabric edge. **D**

Applying a basic centered zipper

The directions that come with most zippers have good diagrams, but some don't come with any directions, so here they are. **Note: Use a ⅜" (9.5mm) seam allowance to install a zipper like this. (The zip pouch is done differently—use the directions for that specific project.)**

1. Mark where the zipper is to go, and stitch the seam closed using a basting stitch. Sew the seam a regular stitch above and below the zipper.

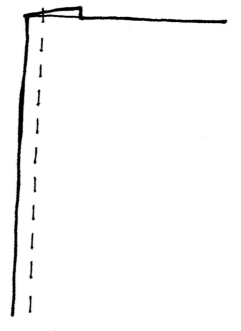

D

2. Switch to a zipper foot. (This will allow you to stitch around the bulky hardware. Don't try to fake it with a regular sewing foot. Trust me, it won't work.) Press the seam flat, and with it facing you, open and pin the zipper face down on top of seam allowance where you have basted. Make sure the zipper is open, and using the basting stitch again, sew the length of one side of the zipper, from bottom to top through the seam allowance only. You can baste the other side of the zipper if you are a nervous Nelly, but you don't have to—one side is enough to keep it in place. **E**

3. Close up the zipper and now, with the right side of the fabric facing you, apply Scotch tape centered over the seam. Sew on either side of the tape. Clever trick, huh?

4. When top stitching, use a regular stitch starting at the zipper bottom. Sew to the top following the edge of the tape. Finish by sewing across the bottom of the zipper. **F**

Machine-made buttonhole

Making a buttonhole is easy by machine. It's best to follow the manual for how to do this on your specific machine. The general idea here is your machine stitches the narrow rectangle for you, but you need to determine the size of the hole based on the button you are using.

1. Determine the buttonhole size by taking a strip of paper and wrapping it around the button; then measure the paper length. **G** Mark this length onto your fabric where you want the hole to go and sew around the mark using your machine's buttonhole stitch. Some machines do this all in one step; others do this in four steps. Test on a scrap piece of fabric first to check size. **H**

2. Cut the buttonhole open by inserting two pins inside either end to act as a barrier so you don't cut through. Snip carefully. Now you are done. Don't fuss about this much, especially if you only have one button. The hole may not look beautiful if it's your first time doing this, but remember—a button will be covering it.

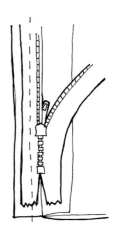

E

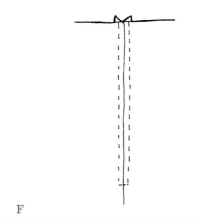

F

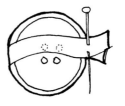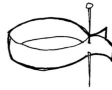

G

H

Sewing on a button

If your button is decorative only, thread your needle with a thick thread or double sewing machine thread and make a knot. Starting from the back of the fabric, bring the needle up where you want it to go and sew through your button, securing through all layers three to four times. Knot in back and clip close to knot. I If your button has a shank, repeat as described above.

If your button actually "buttons" something and has no shank, you need to make a shank. This will prevent it from popping off. This seems fussy, but don't let it intimidate you.

Sew as described above, but when sewing over the top of the button through the holes, insert and sew over a small toothpick or thick hand-sewing needle three to four times. J Then, take the toothpick out and slide the button up in the extra thread. To make the shank, wrap the thread around the extra thread three to four times, then insert the needle through one of the holes to the back of the fabric and tie a knot. K Practice on a scrap of fabric if it's your first time doing this.

Hand-sewn snap

These mini snaps are hidden closures that are hand-sewn on. They are best for delicate projects in which you won't be pulling at them with all your might.

1. Using a double strand of thread, tie a small knot (or use the knotless method) and stitch over the snap edge three to four times all the way around. Tie a knot and bury the tails. Don't sew through all layers; just take tiny stitches through one layer only, so no stitches are seen on the front side.

2. Position the other half of the snap to match up and repeat the process. L

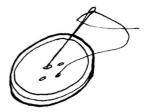

I

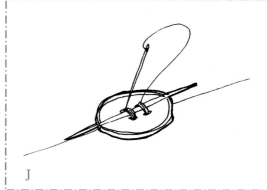

J

K

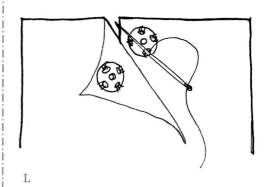

L

Setting a snap

I love using snaps. They are quick and easy. Just buy a pack of snaps and a snap setter. These are not expensive and usually consist of a small metal plug that you whack with a hammer over the snap sandwich you make with the fabric in between the snaps. Use the snap setter instructions and don't try to set the snaps without buying the snap setter, which is normally sold separately. You may be tempted to try it with just a hammer, but it won't work—trust me.

Applying bias trim—three ways

Bias trim is just the best. Because it's cut on the bias, it will follow curves beautifully.

By machine and by hand

This is the traditional way. It takes the longest, but the stitching on the front is completely invisible and the look is gorgeous. Unfold the tape and position the slightly wider side of the tape along the right side edge of fabric. You will notice that one fold is slightly wider than the other and that the narrow side wraps around the back. Using your machine, stitch into place along the entire length of the fabric edge where the trim goes. **M** Fold over the edge onto the backside, and using slip stitch, hand sew into place. **N** Pins will be helpful here. Make sure to use tiny stitches and try to just prick the fabric, not going through all layers. **O** This is the method to use when binding a quilt. For the ending, fold over raw edges away from you before you stitch, so when you turn, the folded edge will be lapped over the top. **P**

By machine zigzag

This is a quick way of applying a bias trim done all by machine. Using a wide zigzag (I prefer a three-way zigzag stitch; most machines have this stitch option), stitch through all layers. **Q** It is much easier to do this without pinning first. This works well on narrow bias trim, about ¼" (6mm). If you use wider trim, widen your zigzag. This method works best when the project is fine, only one layer, not three layers, like on a quilt.

With special foot

You can buy special feet that fit on your sewing machine and feed the trim through, lining it up perfectly so you can use a

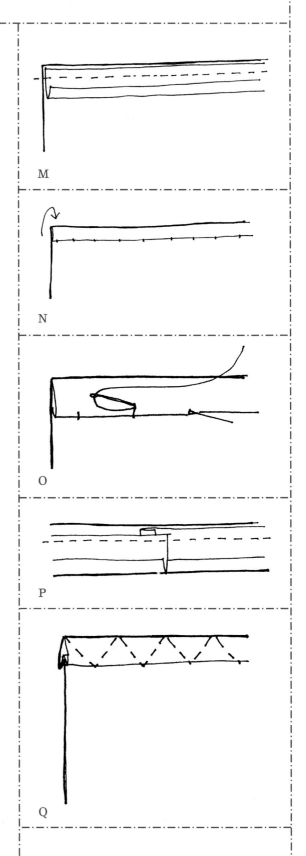

M

N

O

P

Q

tidy straight stitch and hit the tape on both sides every time. If you really like the look of binding and use it a lot, these feet are not very expensive and well worth the investment. The stitches are not invisible, but it's still a neat look. Thinner projects work better for this method as well. Binding a quilt with this method is not a good idea; it's too thick. R

Free-motion quilting

Free-motion quilting is when you lower the feed dogs on your machine and, using a darning foot, move your fabric in any direction to "draw" with the thread. Because you have lowered the feed dogs, which normally feed the fabric for you, you get to move the fabric yourself. If you do this in a jerky, haphazard way, you'll get an irregular stitching line, which is just fine in my book, because I think messy, irregular, free-motion stitching is very cool. Look in your machine's manual and find out how to use a darning foot and how to lower the feed dogs.

I find it easiest to back the fabric I am working on with flannel so I have more to pull with. (I don't use this technique for either quilt in this book, but I do use it as a way to draw with thread to embellish fabric.)

Making bias trim

Bias trim—the old way (which is fine if you aren't making a lot)
You can make your own bias trim. Why would you want to, you ask? Well, fabric choices are my main reason. Also, most premade bias tapes are polyester and stiff and come in limited colors and almost no patterns. The trim is easy to make yourself. You'll need a bias trim–making tool and an iron. Cut your fabric in strips on a 45-degree angle in the width required for the tool you have (each tool only makes one width). Sew the strips together at a 45-degree angle. S Look at the drawing closely here and remember to make the "ears." Iron as you feed the joined strips through the tape maker. The bias trim tools have directions as well, which are helpful to read.

Bias trim—the amazing continuous strip method (which is the way to go in my book)
You start with a square. You will have to experiment with how much this makes, and you might have some extra, but that's okay.

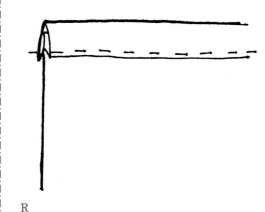

R

When you start to sew, take a little backstitch at the beginning and end of your stitch

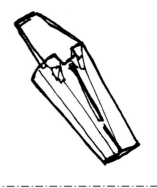

S

To give you an example, a 36" (91cm) square of fabric cut into strips 2¼" (5.5cm) wide (this is unfolded, remember, so when it's folded up it would be much narrower) would make about 13 yards (11.9m) of trim. Wow! That is a lot of trim. This is easier to do than to describe, so just try it on a scrap piece to get a feel for it.

1. Cut your 36" (91cm) square. **T** Cut again corner-to-corner. **U** This needs to be a true square and a true 45-degree cut. Sew together, right sides facing. **V** Notice the top corners overlap slightly—this is important.

2. Using a ruler, draw lines for the overall width of bias trim. **W** Bring the two edges together and position one row below. **X**

3. Match up the rows with pins. Take your time here; this is where it all counts. Sew with right sides together. **Y**

4. Cut on the marked lines to make one continuous strip. **Z** Wasn't that the coolest thing ever? Now feed through your bias trim maker and iron to make your own custom tape.

To make straight binding

This is pieced with straight seams on the straight grain. You can use the bias tape maker the same way, cutting strips of fabric on the straight grain, not diagonal. For a quilt, cut a width of fabric and iron it in half, wrong sides together. Align the raw edges of the folded fabric on top of the right side of the quilt and sew ¼" (6mm) from edge through all layers. Trim raw edge and wrap the binding around to the back of the quilt, pin, and hand sew using a slip stitch and mitered corners.

Making a ruffle

Homemade ruffles are really easy and fun, plus you can use whatever fabric you want. There are several types of ruffles, and one of the easiest is the self-faced ruffle. It uses a bit more fabric, but both sides are finished, so it's perfect for pillows. The following method is not an exact science, so don't get too hung up on the numbers.

1. Determine how much ruffle you will need by measuring the distance the ruffle is going and doubling that number. This measurement is the length of fabric you will need to cut.

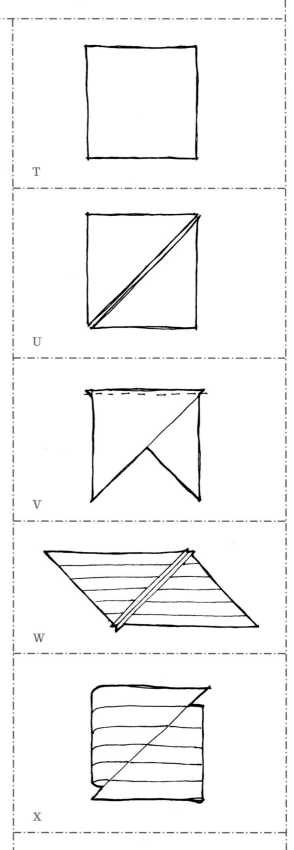

T

U

V

W

X

2. Determine the width by visualizing what will look good and double it. Now add a ½" (13mm) for the seam allowance. For example, if you want your finished ruffle to be 2" (5cm), you will need a strip 4½" (11.5cm) wide.

3. Fold the strip in half lengthwise with right sides facing out. Iron and stitch a basting stitch ¼" (6mm) from the raw edge along the whole length. **AA** Grip the thread on one end and gently tug and pull, letting the strip start to gather on itself. Keep pulling until you get the length you need. **BB** Tie a knot and then evenly distribute the ruffles so there no clumped areas.

When you sew on the ruffle, you will sew just inside of the basting stitch. Remove any basting stitches that do happen to peek out on the front. If you love ruffles, there are sewing machine feet that make the ruffles for you.

Appliqué

Machine appliqué

There are many methods for machine appliqué, and the method I use is a combination of several. I don't like working with fusible interfacings, and I like my appliqué edges neatly tucked in, not raw. Yet I need the speed of using the machine (as opposed to by hand), so this is what I do to get all these results.

1. Trace the finished shape you want to appliqué on the front side of the fabric. I use a water-soluble pen. Then cut around the shape adding about ¼" (6mm) or ½" (13mm), depending on the size of the finished shape. The bigger the shape, the more I allow.

2. Using a small pair of very sharp scissors, make tiny clips about every ¼" (6mm) to ⅛" (3mm), clipping almost to the line you have drawn. This creates tabs so that your shape looks as if it had fringe all the way around it.

3. Finger press the tabs to the back all the way around the shape. You can also use a mini iron for this, but spritz off your marks with cold water before ironing. Fingers work just as well. **CC**

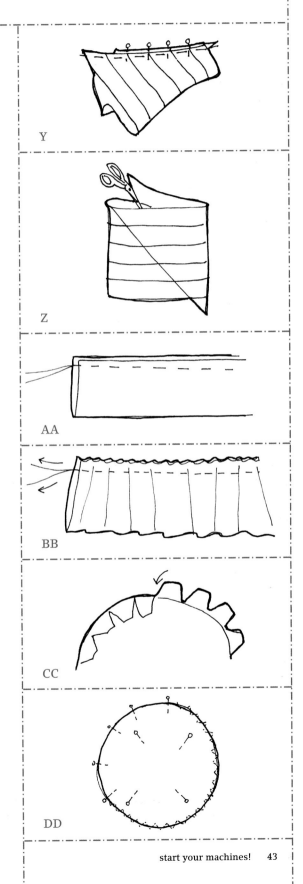

Y

Z

AA

BB

CC

DD

4. Position and pin this shape where you want it to go. Machine zigzag, slowly, keeping all the tabs tucked under. Use a small zigzag and make sure that one of the zags bites into the edge of the shape. **DD** You can use the same color thread or contrasting thread depending on whether or not you want to call attention to the zigzag.

Needle-turn appliqué sewn by hand
I use this method when the pieces are so small machine stitching won't work. This method creates an almost invisible stitch, and I love having the control that comes with hand sewing.

1. On the appliqué fabric, draw your shape to the finished size using a water-soluble pen. Trim outside the line leaving no more than ⅛" to ³⁄₁₆" (3 to 6mm). Carefully finger press the edges along the line you have marked.

2. Pin the shape into position and start sewing using the slip stitch, turning the raw edge of the fabric shape under as you go. Make sure to use the line you have marked as your guide. At corners or tight curves, cut small notches as needed.

3. Continue all the way around, using the needle to fold and tuck the fabric edge under as you sew. Remove marking with cold water when you are done and press. **EE**

Hand sewing

Many sewers steer clear of hand sewing, but hand sewing is not as tedious as you would think. It's important to know the basics, so if you are interested in learning more, there are books and entire crafts devoted to hand sewing. It's a wonderful way to add embellishments, lettering, decorative lines, and custom artwork to any project. **Tip: If your thread is getting tangled a lot as you stitch by hand, run the thread over some beeswax.**

Tying a knot
Wrap the thread around your finger two to three times, roll it onto itself, and pull the thread off and away from your finger.

MAKE YOUR SEWING MACHINE WORK FOR YOU

Your machine is supposed to help you, not hinder you. Most basic machines come with special feet to make tasks easier, such as a zipper foot, a buttonhole foot, a walking foot, and sometimes a foot for thick fabrics. You can also buy specialty feet for your machine, such as a ruffle foot, a baby hem foot, an invisible zipper foot, and many more. Try out all the tools your machine has to offer; they are made to make your life easier.

Many machines also can sew a variety of decorative stitches that are really fun and easy to use. Try adding some to your projects, but in small amounts. A little decorative stitching can go a long way, unless you are making something involved in yodeling.

EE

I like to bend the rules. Bend, but not break.

The Basics: Handy sewing techniques to help you make your projects

Knotless start

This trick is wonderful for adding handwork when you can't get to the back of the fabric, like on a stuffed animal or a finished pillow.

1. Thread the needle with a double strand of thread, but thread the two tails through the eye, not the folded edge.

2. Take a small stitch and pull the needle through the loop. Start your hand sewing. Finish by burying the tails. **FF**

Burying the tails

This hides the tails of thread when you are sewing a stuffed object.

1. When you are done sewing, make a small knot through the last stitch. Do this again and then stick the needle under the fabric as far as you can reach.

2. Pull the thread tight enough to cause the fabric to gather a bit and trim the thread tails as close as you can to the fabric. Let go. The tails will sink under the fabric.

Running stitch

This "in-and-out" stitch makes a dashed line. It can also be used as a gathering stitch when knotted on one end and pulled taut. You can just wing it here if you want a primitive look, but with practice, this is a very tidy stitch that looks nice if the thread on top of "the dash" is about twice the length of the space between the stitches. **GG**

Backstitch

This stitch is a bit of forward and backward to create a solid line. It's easier to look at the drawing here than to read about it. **HH**

French knot

This is a decorative knot made by wrapping the thread around the needle and pulling it through to the back. Again, it's easier to look at the drawing. **II**

Slip stitch

This almost invisible stitch is invaluable. Use it to apply bindings and appliqué. Just remember to carry the thread in between the folded edge and come up in a vertical line. Prick the fabric you are sewing onto and then carry the length again in the fold. **JJ**

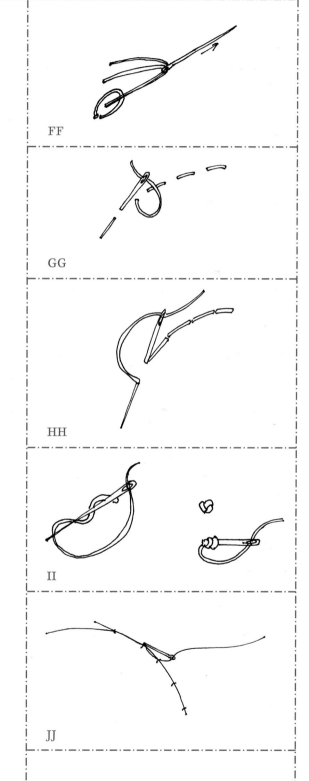

FF

GG

HH

II

JJ

Mixed media fun on fabric

I love drawing, painting, and stamping on fabric. I suggest using freezer paper on the back of fabric for tracing templates, and the same logic applies to mixed media. When you iron freezer paper to the back of the fabric first, the fabric will accept more of the paint or ink. Leave the freezer paper on until the paint or ink dries and then peel it off and heat set. When you are trying these techniques, remember the beauty of them is that they look hand applied. If they look too perfect, they will lose that artsy feel. Plus, trying to make them look perfect can cause a lot of frustration. So try to get a clear image, but don't worry if there are bumps or some irregularities. They will only add to the charm.

Ironing freezer paper to fabric

Freezer paper is not waxed paper; it has a thin plastic coating on one side. (Not all grocery stores carry freezer paper anymore, so you might have to order it online or check at a fabric shop.) Use a hot, dry iron to press it to the back of your fabric with the shiny, coated side of the freezer paper facing the fabric.

Fabric markers

I like brush-tip markers, and the best kinds have both the brush tips and the normal tips. Make sure they are made especially for fabric. You might have to order these online or from a catalog. I iron on freezer paper first, and if I want to just doodle, I do this with a water-soluble pen. Then, I trace with the fabric marker, let it dry, spray off the water-soluble marker, and heat set. I especially like Micron Pigma markers for black ink and small lettering.

Fabric paint

Use the same technique as above. There are inexpensive fabric paints that you can get at the craft store. I'd recommend staying away from these and using the high-quality kinds from online shops and catalogs. The problem with most fabric paint has been that it lies on top of the fabric and leaves a hard plastic feel. There are fabric paints available now that are almost indistinguishable from dyes. They are amazing and worth trying. **Tip: If the paint is too thick, thin it with colorless extenders, as opposed to water; otherwise it can bleed.**

WHEN BUYING FABRICS, THINK LIKE A HIPPIE

I almost exclusively choose natural fibers when I buy fabric. This is not just for environmental reasons but also for tactile preference as well. I just love the way cotton, wool, silk, and linen sew and feel and breathe and move. I strongly recommend you use 100 percent natural fibers for these projects. They will press easily and smoothly, which is so helpful. Man-made blends tend to fight the iron. I use new and vintage fabrics, and once you work with fabric a bit, you can tell whether it's a natural fiber. If you are in doubt, or if it's a vintage fabric and hard to tell, a small flame will melt a blend, but cotton will singe. I don't recommend lighting fabric on fire in a store, however; do this at home only.

If you can, buy the best you can afford. High-quality cottons are really worth it. If you think about how much fabric you will need for these projects (not much) and then calculate how much money you will save by getting cheaper fabric, you may save a dollar or two. But you can't achieve the feel of a finely made fabric. Look for fabric at a local quilt shop or fabric store first, and if you can't find what you want, there are several online shops that will sell you fabrics that you never even knew you *had* to have. Try vintage fabric. Old table linens are a great choice. Although you will be tempted to make projects from thrifted bed sheets, be really careful. These are almost always a blend of cotton and polyester and are really hard to iron. They were made to be "no-iron" sheets, so when you do try to iron them, you might be in for a fight.

The paint will soak though the freezer paper but won't bleed unless you are painting in really large areas. Only painted lines are used for the projects in this book. If you are filling in shapes with paint, you might need to experiment more and have extra fabric on hand. Heat set when you are all done, if it is required. And use a good brush to paint with.

Rubber stamps

You can carve your own designs (look online for a ton of info on rubber-stamp carving) or you can use a purchased stamp. I have had only marginal success with fabric ink stamp pads, so I usually use the brush tip of a fabric marker to "paint" the ink directly onto the stamp. Then, I stamp on the fabric, which has been ironed onto freezer paper. Then, I fill in any light area with the brush tip on the marker. Some colors work better than others, and line art works better than areas with a lot of color. Experiment with your markers first to see.

THE JOY OF PREWASH FABRIC

Prewash your fabric, especially if you think the finished item will ever need to be washed, which most likely it will. I prewash everything because I really like the way a fabric feels after it's been washed. Since I tend to like a more handmade look, I try to make the fabric look less crisp and new, as if it were from my vintage stash. Dry as you would dry the finished item, which probably means in the dryer. You will get some shrinkage, so keep this in mind when you are buying the fabric. Buy a quarter-yard extra if you are worried about it.

part 2 *bend-the-rules projects*

gifts: to give away or keep for yourself

The Zip Pouch

The zip pouch is one of the handiest little bags to know how to sew. You can keep pencils, make-up, tools, notions, gifts, and buttons—anything you want—in there. I make several at a time. Try using iron vinyl on the lining fabric to make the inside water-proof. There are many ways to sew these zip pouches, but my favorite way is to hand sew in the lining. Although it takes a bit longer, it will always turn out perfectly. Because you can see exactly where you are stitching, the zipper always stays nice and flat.

MATERIALS

Outside fabric: (2) 5½" × 7" (14 × 18cm) pieces
Lining fabric: (2) 5½" × 7" (14 × 18cm) pieces
Iron vinyl (optional)
Zipper: about 7" (18cm) long
Ribbons or trims (optional)

SEAM ALLOWANCE: ¼" (6mm)

1. If you want to have ribbons or trims on your pouch, add that now. Cut out all your rectangles, and on the outer fabric place ribbon and edge stitch down.

2. Make a bow by stitching across a loop of ribbon. A Wrap a small bit of ribbon around the loop to make the "knot." B Hand stitch closed. C Stitch ribbon across front fabric along the ribbon's top and bottom edge. Hand stitch bow on. D

3. Fold over about ¼" (6mm) on the top edges of the front fabric pieces and align next to the zipper teeth. Pin into place and, using a zipper foot, stitch to the top of the zipper. The right side of the zipper should be facing up. E

4. Open the zipper halfway down, and with right sides facing, sew the sides and bottom of the outer front and back of the pouch together. If the zipper is too long, just sew straight through. By doing that, you will create a shorter zipper. F Trim extra zipper length off, if you have any. Turn inside out and completely open the zipper.

5. If you want to use vinyl on your fabric lining, do that now—just follow the vinyl directions. With right sides facing, sew around the sides and the bottom lining. Turn, press. G Fold down ¼" (6mm) on top edge.

6. Insert lining into zip pouch and pin just under the zip-per teeth. Using a sharp needle and a slip stick, hand stitch into place on the zipper tape only, making sure not to stitch all the way to the front. You need to do this only on the front and back. Don't worry about trying to get the lining hand-stitched under the zipper stop and the pull tab—you won't see that part and this will be plenty strong. H

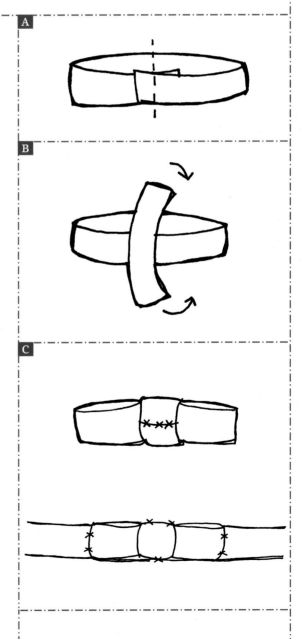

A

B

C

The Zip Pouch

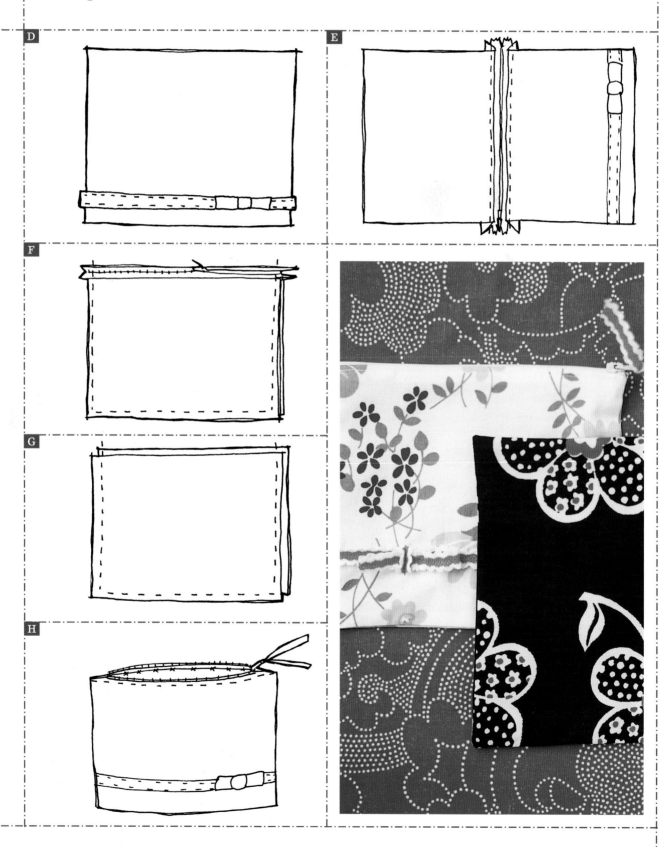

Whipping together a homemade gift is easy and fun, and it's so much better than going to the mall.

Simple Tote

A contrasting back, lining, pocket, and handles make this simple tote look modern and bold. Don't be afraid to just do your own thing. I used a single vintage linen napkin with apples on it for the front fabric; I only had one, and I had to use it on something!

MATERIALS

Pattern fabric:
   Outside front: (1) 10½" × 9" (26.5 × 23cm) piece
   Inside pocket: (1) 7" × 4¾" (18 × 12cm) piece
   Short strap: (1) 3" × 8" (7.5 × 20.5cm) piece
Solid fabric:
   Lining and back: (3) 10½" × 9" (26.5 × 23cm) pieces
   Long strap: (1) 13" × 16" (7.5 × 40.5cm) piece
Cotton flannel facing fabric: (2) 10½" × 9" (26.5 × 23cm) pieces

SEAM ALLOWANCE: ¼" (6mm)

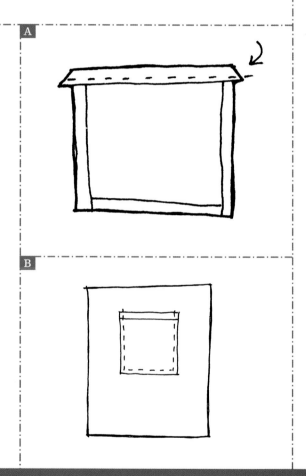

1. Cut out all pieces. Make pocket by stitching top edge down and folding over remaining three edges. **A** Pin onto lining piece and stitch on sides and bottom. **B**

2. With right sides together, stitch sides and bottom of outer fabrics of the bag. **C** Stitch across corners to make a box bottom. Trim excess off corner, turn, and press. **D**

3. Lay out facing and lining fabrics, right sides facing, and stitch the two sides and the bottom. **E** Stitch across corners, and trim and press. **D**

4. Make your handles by turning your strips under ⅛" (3mm) on the edge and pressing. **F** Fold in half lengthwise and edge stitch. **G**

5. With right sides together, place the lining bag into the outer bag and pin the handles in place, facing down. Stitch around top, leaving an opening to turn. **H**

6. Turn and edge stitch around top. **I** Press. To hold, insert the longer handle through the shorter one.

HINTS AND TIPS

- This is one of those projects that is easier to do than to read about. You may make mistakes the first time around, but after that, it will be really easy.

- This project uses very little fabric, making it the perfect project for fabric scraps.

- This bag is easy to customize. You can use same-sized handles, if you prefer, and experiment with the overall size. Just make sure all your pieces are the same size to begin with.

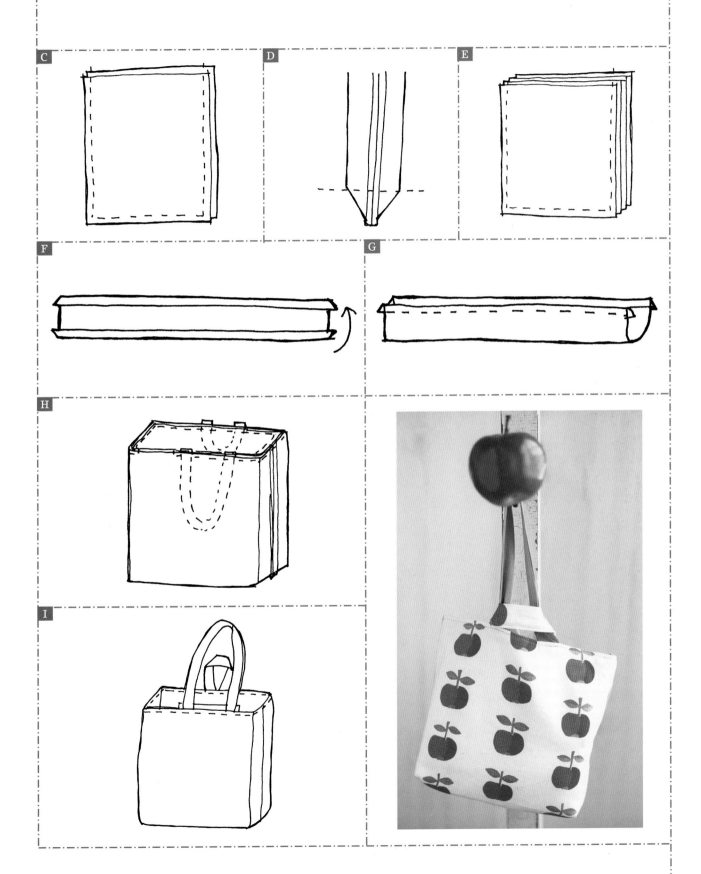

Heidi Headband

This quick and easy headband is made with ribbon and backed with linen. It ties in the back with twill tape for easy adjustments. You can use an embroidered ribbon, but it would be just as lovely with a velvet or silk ribbon. This is a great project to use up short lengths of ribbon too pretty to throw away. You will have made ten of these before you even know it. They are addictive.

MATERIALS

1"- (2.5cm-) wide fabric ribbon: (1) 18" (4.5cm) length
Linen fabric for back: (1) 3½" x 19" (9 x 48.5cm) piece
½" (13mm) twill tape: 22" (56cm) cut into two equal lengths

SEAM ALLOWANCE: ¼" (6mm)

1. Cut the linen strip and fold up the ends with a tiny fold. Iron and stitch. A

2. Fold the strip in half lengthwise, right side facing in, and stitch ¼" (6mm) along top edge. B Turn tube inside out using your bodkin to help you. Press.

3. Insert twill tape into each tube end and stitch shut. C

4. Edge stitch the ribbon on the front, pivoting at one end, and stitch back up the other side. Fold up the ends of the ribbon with a tiny fold; iron and stitch. Press. D

HINTS AND TIPS

- You can make your own ribbon out of fabric by ironing under the raw edges of a fabric strip and applying as if it were ribbon.

- Customize the width by using a narrower ribbon and reducing the backing piece accordingly.

- This is a great project for young children. They can pick the ribbon, you make the band, and then they can add buttons, trims, or felt flowers. This is a great activity for a birthday party. Just complete step 3 before the party and then have the girls pick out the finishing touches.

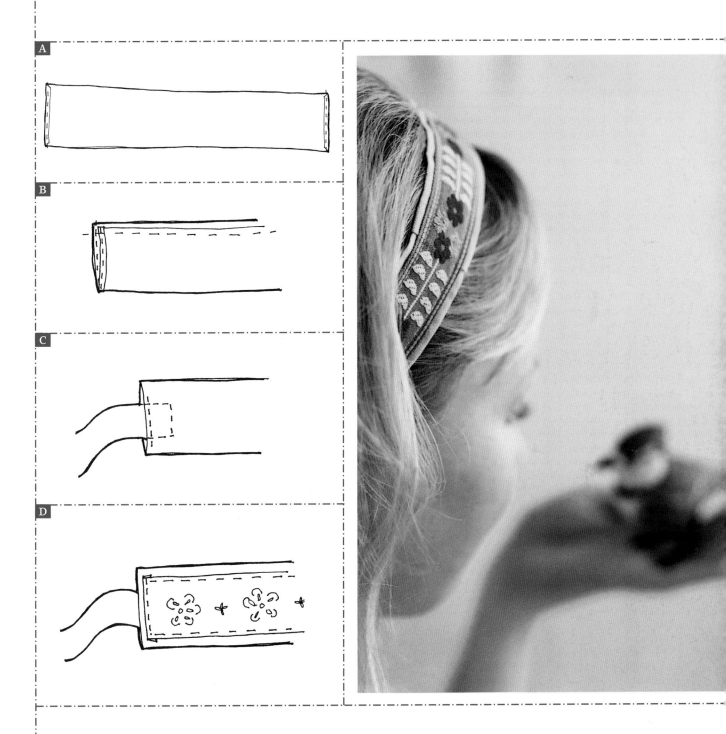

A

B

C

D

The No Cash Wallet

Although I love the feel of a crisp new dollar bill, I am the card-carrying type. I never have cash and don't carry a checkbook, so I need very little from my wallet except a couple pockets, good looks, and a sunny disposition. Add a clever snap under the button (no button holes!) and we are ready to go shopping.

MATERIALS
Outside fabric and pockets: (1) 8" × 12" (20.5 × 30.5cm) piece
Lining fabric: (1) 5" × 12" (12.5 × 30.5cm) piece
Cotton flannel facing: (1) 5" × 12" (12.5 × 30.5cm) piece
Button
Sewn-in tiny snap

SEAM ALLOWANCE: ¼" (6mm)

PATTERN: page 126

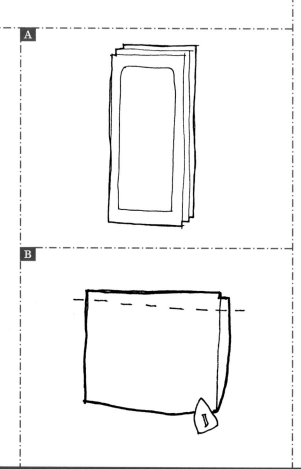

1. Cut out the pattern pieces. A

2. Make the two pockets. Iron one in half, right sides together, and stitch across one long edge. Turn and iron flat. This is the center pocket. B The other pocket you just iron in half, right sides out. C

3. Pin both pockets to the lining piece. Edge stitch center pocket to lining piece at bottom of pocket only. D

4. Lay out the facing piece, then the lining and the outer fabric, right sides facing. Stitch all the way around, catching the pockets as you sew. E Leave an opening to turn. Turn and press.

5. Edge stitch around the entire wallet, stitching the opening closed as you go. Sew two seams across the wallet where it will fold up. F

6. Hand sew in tiny snap, and then on the outside front add a button. This option is decorative; the snap is what keeps the wallet closed. G Fill with your plastic cards and go shopping!

HINTS AND TIPS
- A large-scale fabric is bold and eye catching, especially on the inside pockets framed with a solid fabric.
- This is designed to fit the cards well, so they don't slide out. If your pieces are a bit off your cards might not fit. Check as you go, making sure you leave enough room to fit them in.

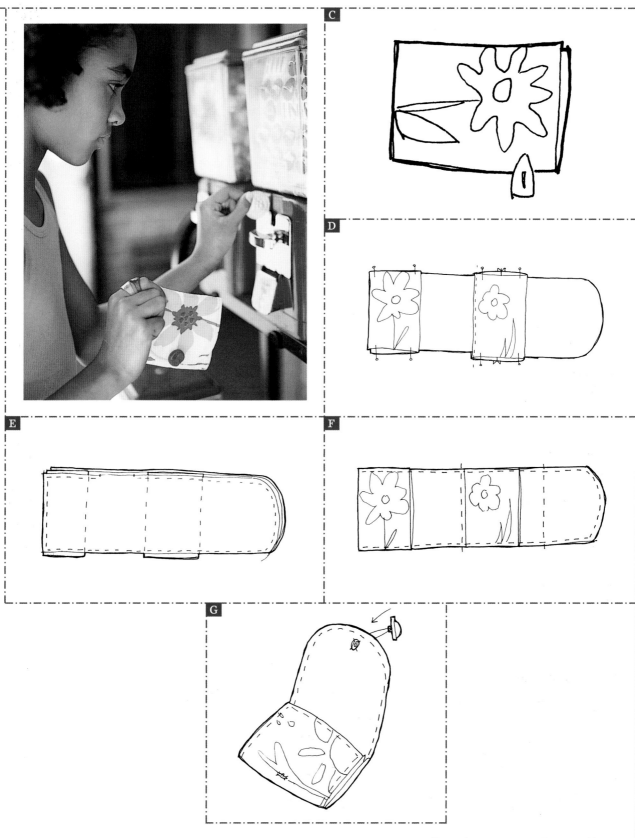

WHAT KIND OF CRAFTER ARE YOU?

As in any complex relationship, we keep making the same mistakes over and over in our crafts. Here's a tongue-in-cheek guide to the creativity personality types. Knowing mine really helped me reduce the amount of gratuitous cursing in the craft room.

The Perfectionist

Do you tend to focus on the details? Are crisp ironing and perfect seams your calling card? If you tend to go pretty slow and take out a lot of seams, you may be a Perfectionist crafter. The upside of this approach is that your workmanship is usually amazing. The downside is that you can burn out really easily and start piling up unfinished projects. The solution? Have some fun, and try this exercise: give someone a less-than-perfect sewn item as a gift. Yes, you can do this. When the recipient shrieks with delight and gushes over your creation, you can breathe easy, because they didn't even notice the flaws that you were so worried about, did they? Okay, now do this again. And again. You get the picture.

The Miser

Can you work miracles reusing fabric? Do you thrift like a demon and have an amazing knack for sensing a yard sale a mile away? Misers can see project potential in cast-off items and can make gifts for pennies. The flip side can be a tendency not to cut enough fabric (which is my own personal downfall, too). If you thrift fabric, often you have little control of the quantity. So you tend to have not quite enough. (Or you are being a miser, and don't want to use it all.) Misers will undercut the fabric, making it stretch as far as it can go. But scrimping on seam allowances comes at a price: no matter how clever you are, you cannot make up for not having enough fabric. Attention Misers: Stop waiting for the "perfect project," keep your fabric stash in check, and don't buy fabric only because it's on sale. Buy what you love—and use it liberally.

The Artist

If you are known to all of your friends as a crazy crafter who flies by the seat of her pants, you fit the Artist profile. Artists make imaginative creations and work from inspiration, photos, or their own crazy brains: they sew when inspiration strikes. They think, "I can make that," and dive right in. The result is unexpected and one of a kind. Some of the absolute best sewing projects can be made this way. But using a technique once or twice, usually with methods you have made up, can cause problems: because there is no plan or pattern to start with, the projects can easily get out of control, become frustrating, and, ultimately, be left abandoned. When Artist crafters come up with a masterpiece, it can be impossible to re-create (usually because part of the design was working around an unexpected turn the project took). To follow a pattern from start to finish, you need to trick yourself: try pretending you have never sewn before. Pretend you are a brand new sewer and master some basic skills with confidence. This can really help.

The Speed Demon

Speed Demons are the opposite of Perfectionists. If you get a rush out of doing a lot of sewing in a short amount of time, and instead of making one bag in a weekend, you make eight—guess what? You are a Speed Demon. Demons love giving gifts and really are good at using the machine and tools to their best advantage. They go with the flow, don't get hung up on the minor mistakes, and have fun looking at the pile of creations they have made. But sometimes this way of sewing can produce some lazy habits. Sloppy ironing (or no ironing), pieces of sewn-off grain, and odd fabric choices are some common culprits. Although you don't want to get too detail-focused, you don't want to make something that looks completely, well, half-baked. If the project won't lie flat, looks odd, or is otherwise funky, then slow down, Speed Demon! Curves ahead!

Artsy Clutch

This quick and easy clutch is really just a soft bag that folds over onto itself and buttons closed. The look will change drastically with the fabric you choose. After you make one and learn the technique, have fun making different sizes.

MATERIALS
Outside fabric: (2) 8" × 9½" (20.5 × 24cm) pieces
Lining fabric: (2) 8" × 9½" (20.5 × 24cm) pieces
Cotton flannel facing fabric: (2) 8" × 9½" (20.5 × 24cm) pieces
Big vintage button
Elastic cording
Fabric paint or fabric markers

SEAM ALLOWANCE: ¼" (6mm)

TEMPLATE: page 127

1. Cut the rectangles out of your fabric. Using the template, paint or draw on your fabric. Let dry and heat set. With right sides together, sew around sides and bottom of outside fabric; turn and press. **A**

2. Lay out lining fabric and cotton flannel. From bottom to top: flannel fabric; lining, right sides facing up; lining, wrong sides facing up; flannel fabric. Stitch both sides and bottom of bag. Turn and press. **B**

3. With right sides together, place the lining bag into the outer bag and pin elastic cord. Stitch around top, leaving opening to turn insides out. Turn and press. **C**

4. Edge stitch around top, catching opening closed. **D** Fold over top and make button placement. Before you sew the button on, put some stuff in the clutch and fold again; adjust the button placement, making sure you have enough room to close it. **E**

HINTS AND TIPS
- This basic clutch is a great way to learn how to line and face a bag. Once you have it down here, you can use the technique on the other projects really easily.

- Try this in a silk or linen to make a really nice evening clutch. The button you choose can be simple or flashy; experiment with the different options. Bridesmaids would love these.

- The lining shows in the design, so a fun look would be to use an understated outer fabric and then have a really bright lining peek out.

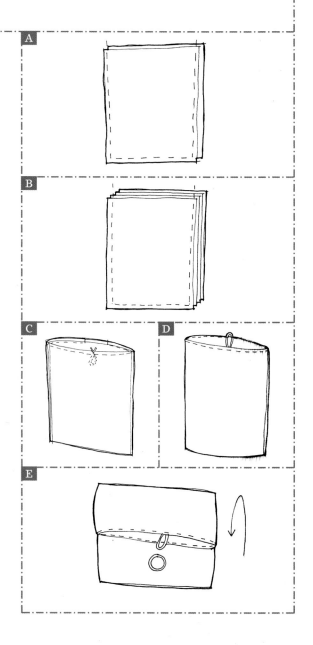

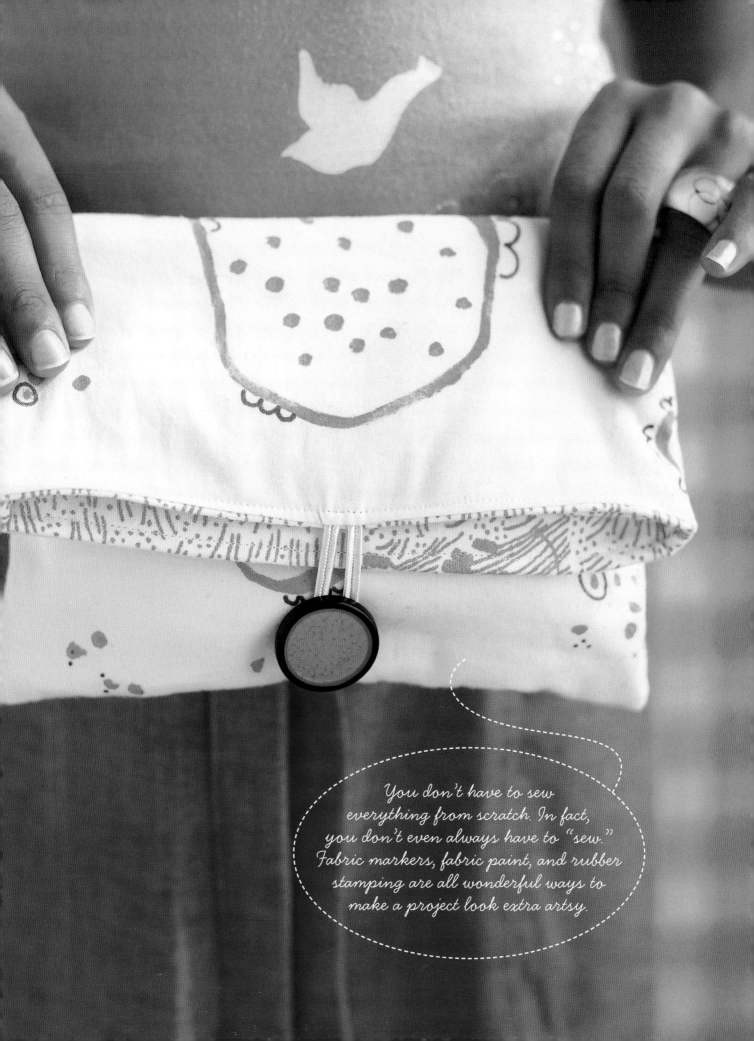

You don't have to sew
everything from scratch. In fact,
you don't even always have to "sew."
Fabric markers, fabric paint, and rubber
stamping are all wonderful ways to
make a project look extra artsy.

Charming Handbag

This small, elegant handbag is sweet and lovely. Just big enough for your essentials, it quietly steals the show. The handles are threaded through a casing in the lining, so when you pull them, the bag gathers slightly. The velvet ribbon is optional, but really, how could you leave it off?

MATERIALS

Outside fabric and handles: (2) 13" × 13" (33 × 33cm) pieces
Handle fabric: (1) 2"× 22" (5.1 × 55.9cm) piece
Lining fabric and casing fabric: (2) 13" × 13" (33 × 33cm) pieces
Casing fabric: (2) 1½" × 6" (3.8 × 15.2cm) pieces
Cotton flannel facing fabric: (2) 13" × 11" (33 × 28cm) pieces
⅞" (2.2cm) velvet ribbon: about 18" (45.5cm) length

SEAM ALLOWANCE: ¼" (6mm)

PATTERN: page 128

1. Cut out all the pattern pieces for the bag on the fold of the fabric. A

2. Sew the two notches together on all pieces, outer fabric, lining, and facing. This will be six pieces in all. Iron flat. B

3. Make the ribbon "bow" by folding the ribbon in a loop. C Sew across the middle. Wrap a small piece of ribbon around the middle, making a hand stitch in back. D

4. On the outer front fabric, pin the velvet ribbon. Edge stitch ribbon close to top and bottom edge. Hand stitch the bow to the front of the bag. E

5. Sew together the two outer fabric pieces right sides together on the side and bottom seams. F

6. Sew the lining and facing pieces together. G

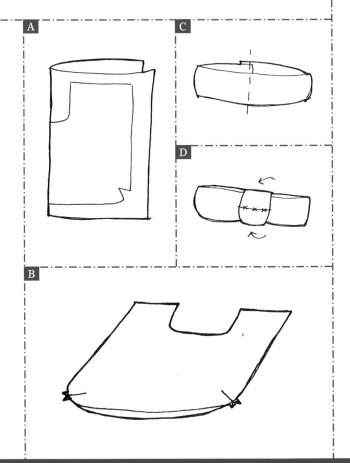

HINTS AND TIPS

- This bag uses a slightly different shape to make a flat bottom bag. It's a nice variation to know when designing your own handbags.

- Try a contrasting handle.

- A bigger shape and longer handle would make this bag a great tote.

7. Make the casing for the handles by folding the strips down once about ¼" (6mm) on the short edges and edge stitch. Then iron down about ¼" (6mm) on the top and bottom. H

8. Pin casing to lining about ½" (13mm) from the top edge and stitch top and bottom edge only. The handles will slide through the openings on the sides. I, J

9. Place the lining bag inside the outer bag, right sides together, and stitch along the top edge, leaving an opening for turning. K

10. Turn, press, and edge stitch around the top opening. L

11. Make handles by ironing the handle strip down ¼" (6mm) from top and bottom edge. M Then fold in half again and edge stitch. Press. N

12. Thread handle through the casing and then sew closed, rotating the seamed part into the casing where it remains hidden. O, P

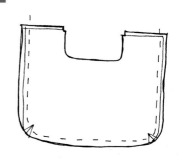

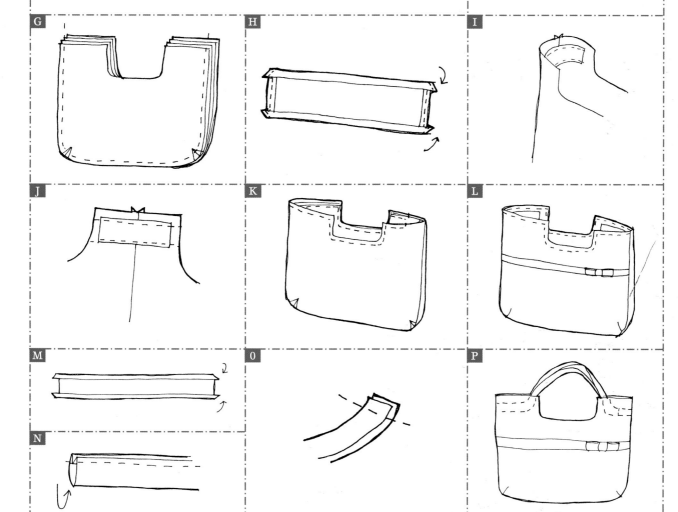

Pleated Beauty Handbag

This understated handbag is just what you need to feel special. Bright peek-a-boo pleats give this linen bag a bit of sass, and it's roomy enough to hold your wallet, craft supplies, and a book. The artsy hand stitching combined with free-motion quilting is optional, but it's a perfect-sized project on which to try these techniques for the first time. The handles have contrasting linings, and there is a contrasting inside pocket great for keys and a phone. The rigid bottom helps it retain its shape so you can really stuff it full.

While these steps aren't hard, there are a lot of them. Give yourself plenty of time to work on this project. Work in stages, doing only a few steps at a time so you don't get burned out or rush the details. There is a big payoff in the end. You will love this bag!

MATERIALS

Outside bag fabric and lining fabric:
- (2) 10½" × 15½" (26.5 × 39.5cm) pieces for outside of bag
- (4) 4½" × 15½" (11.5 × 39.5cm) pieces for outside of bag
- (2) 1½" × 22" (3.8 × 56cm) pieces for outside straps
- (2) 22" × 15½" (56 × 39.5cm) pieces for lining

Contrasting fabric:
- (4) 2½" × 15½" (6.5 × 39.5cm) pieces for pleats
- (1) 10" × 9" (25.4 × 23cm) piece for inside pocket
- (2) 1½" × 22" (3.8 × 56cm) pieces for inside strap linings

Facing fabric (cotton flannel):
- (2) 15½" × 22" (56 × 39.5cm) pieces
- (2) 16" × 5" (40.5 × 12.5cm) pieces (for making the rigid interfacing pillow)

Rigid interfacing: (1) 15" × 4" (38 × 10cm) piece
Embroidery floss
Water-soluble pen
2 vintage buttons

SEAM ALLOWANCE: ¼" (6mm)

TEMPLATE: page 129

1. Cut out the rectangles for the outer fabric first. Mark design for machine and hand stitching, using the template (or just make up your own). You will want to do any embellishments on the bag now. Free-motion quilt and hand stitch using a running stitch and add the buttons. If you are doing your own design, remember to keep the bottom 3" (7.5cm) of this piece plain because this will become the bottom of the bag. A

2. Cut out contrasting pocket piece. Turn up the three edges ¼" (6mm) and press. Turn down ½" (13mm) on top, stitch, and press. B Lay out as follows: flannel facing; lining, right side up; and then pocket, right side up. Stitch the sides and bottom of the pocket down through all the thicknesses. C

3. Stitch together the contrasting fabric strips (for pleats) and the outside bag pieces. D Repeat for the back of the bag. (There is no embellishment on the back of the bag.) Check to make sure your fronts and backs are the same size and trim if necessary. Lay out the cotton flannel and lining pieces (one will have the pocket), again trimming if necessary—they should all be the same size. Baste the two cotton flannel pieces to the wrong sides of the two lining pieces and pretend it is one piece from now on. Mark the pleats on the lining fabric and mark where you will keep the side open for turning inside out.

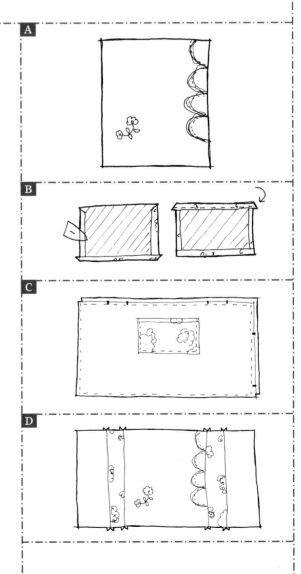

4. Sew the pleats by matching the edges of the contrasting fabric together and sewing down 2" (5cm) from top edge. E Repeat for remaining three pleats. Press. On the right side of the front and back, top stitch on the four pleats. F Sew the pleats on the lining where you marked before the same way as above. The cotton flannel will be folded in there, too; just pretend it's all one piece. You don't have to top stitch the pleats in the lining. G

5. With right sides facing together, sew around the two sides and bottom of outside bag fabric. Repeat with the lining fabric, but make sure to leave it open where marked. H Fold the bag as shown and stitch 1¾" (4.5cm) from each corner to form the bottom of the bag. Trim off corner. Repeat on the lining fabric bag. I

6. Cut the rigid interfacing and two flannel pieces. Make sure it fits in the bottom of the bag, trimming if necessary. Sandwich the rigid interfacing in the middle of two cotton flannel pieces and press following the manufacturer's directions. J Stitch around all four edges. Trim and then hand stitch a few times to the bottom of the bag only on the cotton flannel side of the lining in the four corners. K

7. Make the straps by ironing up ¼" (6mm) on top and bottom of the linen strips. Do the same with the contrasting strips, but turn up just a bit more. Lay the contrasting strip on top of the linen strip, so the right sides are facing out. Edge stitch on either side of the strap. L Pin straps to top outside of bag, just to the inside of each pleat. Make sure to pin the straps with the linen side of the strap facing the linen bag front. M

8. With right sides together, pin the two bags together. If the lining is too big, stitch a bit into the side seams to make it smaller. If the outer bag is too big, do the same. Take your time and make sure they fit together to avoid the dreaded puckers and unwanted pleats. Stitch around the top, catching the straps. M Trim if you need to, and turn inside out through the side opening. Press the top edge and edge stitch around the top. N Hand sew the opening in the lining on the inside.

HINTS AND TIPS

- Skip all the front embellishment if you want to. A plain fabric with a bright pleat looks lovely, as does the reverse combination. You could also add a brooch, felt flower, or some other jewelry to the front of this bag if you don't want to do the handwork.

- Don't get too bogged down by the measurements in the project. The key is to make sure all the pieces are the same size as each other and the outside pleats are in roughly the same location.

- Make sure to leave a big enough side opening in the lining for turning inside out. The rigid interfacing needs a lot of room to go through. You can machine stitch this closed when you are done if you don't want to do it by hand.

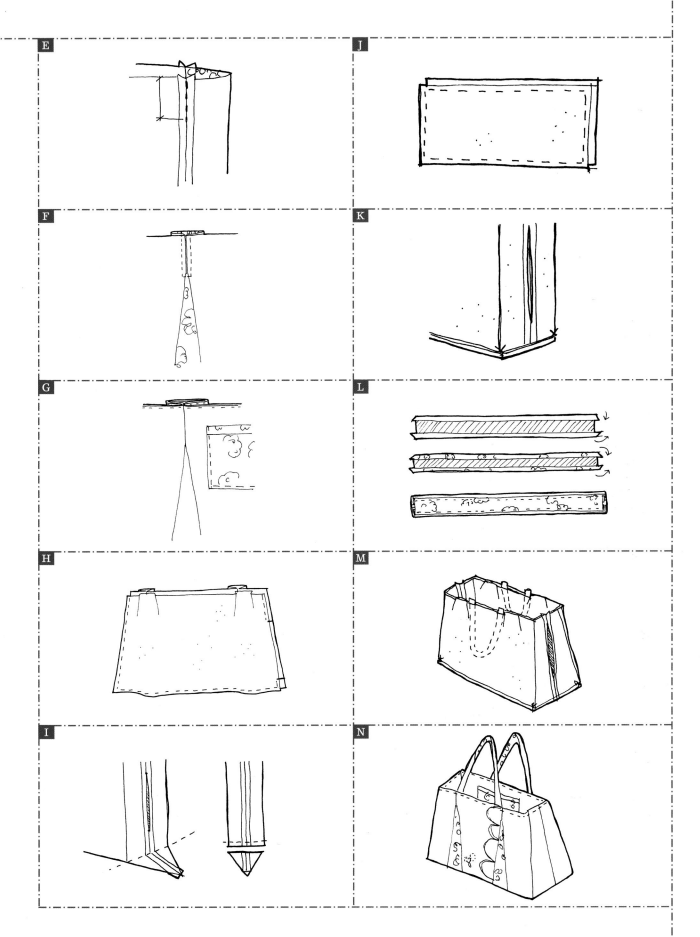

The Accessorized Canine (The Dog Collar)

This easy collar for small or large dogs will have you thinking crazy thoughts like, "Maybe I should make a collar for Sparky to match my skirt today." You can find collar clips and D-rings at the sewing store in the notions section. They are usually plastic and heavy duty. Make sure to add the D-ring, because that's what you want to hang the ID tags from, and a leash can attach to it as well.

MATERIALS

Clip closure: ¾" to 1½" (2 to 3.8cm), depending on the size of the dog
Collar fabric: 4" × 22-ish" (10 × 56-ish cm), depending on clip size
Twill tape: about 2" (5cm) length
D-ring: 1" (2.5cm) wide
Safety pins

SEAM ALLOWANCE: ¼" (6mm)

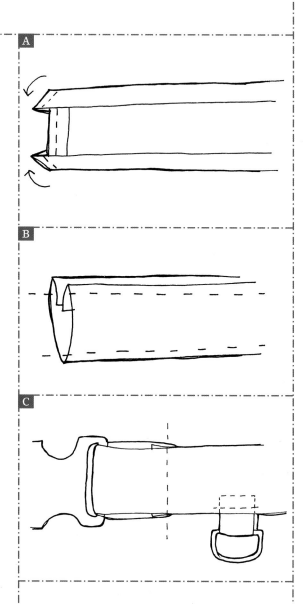

1. Measure your dog's neck and add about 5"–7" (12.5–18cm). Determine the width by measuring the opening in your clip and double it. Then add ½" (13mm) to this amount. For example, the blue collar clip (opposite page) is 1" (2.5cm) wide, so I cut a 2½" (6.3cm) wide piece. Fold over ¼" (6mm) edge on one short end and press. Top stitch. A

2. Turn over ¼" (6mm) of top and bottom edge of strip and press. Fold it in half and press. Edge stitch both edges. Now one end will be finished and one end will have raw edges. B

3. Thread the strap through the clasp of the clip, safety pin in place, and wrap around your dog's neck. If it's way too long, cut some excess off the raw edge of the collar.

4. Unpin and now sew onto the clasp. Take the raw edge end and thread through the clasp turning the raw end under and stitching across. Cut a small piece of twill tape and slide the D-ring on. On the backside, stitch across the tape ends several times to securely attach the tape to the collar. Thread the finished collar edge through the other end of the clip and tighten as needed to fit your dog's neck. C

Cat Tuffet in a Basket

Every time I get out my fabrics, my cats come running. So to make them happy (and make me less crazy), I made them their own fabric basket to sleep in. This wicker serving tray, from the local import store, is lined with a round cushion that zips off for easy washing. A catnip mouse is tied on the basket for extra incentive to stay off my sewing table.

There are a lot of instructions here, but not because this project is hard—it's not. But you are going to use your basket as a template to make the pillow, and since baskets come in all shapes, I am giving you the long version so you can customize it.

MATERIALS

Pillow fabric: (2) 22" x 22" (56 x 56cm) pieces for a 16" (40.5cm) diameter basket (about 4" [10cm] larger than the overall size of your basket, plus a bit extra for the catnip fish)

Cotton flannel for pillow insert: (2) 22" x 22" (56 x 56cm) pieces for a 16" (40.5cm) diameter basket (about 4" [10cm] larger than the overall size of your basket)

Poly-fill

9" (23cm) zipper to match fabric

Ribbon for catnip mouse

Catnip

Wicker serving tray or shallow basket (could be rectangular) The one shown here is 16" (40.5cm) in diameter, but consider your cat's size and choose the best fit.

SEAM ALLOWANCE: ¼" (6mm)

PATTERN: page 130

1. Get your basket and place it on top of the cotton flannel fabric. Trace. A Now add about 1" (2.5cm) to this circle and mark again. This larger circle is your stitching line. Cut outside this line, leaving about a ¼" (6mm) seam allowance. B

2. Cut the pillow top and the remaining cotton flannel piece this size as well. Make your pillow insert by stitching around the 2 flannel pieces, leaving an opening. Turn, and stuff with poly-fill. C (Make this pillow soft, not firm. Kitty should sink into the pillow.) Machine stitch opening closed. Put this in the tray to see how it fits.

3. Make the pillow bottom with the zipper. Using the pillow top fabric as your template, fold the top in half and place on fold of bottom fabric, adding about ½" (13mm) on the fold side (to allow for zipper seam allowance) D and cut out bottom pieces by cutting around the half circle and cutting down the fold.

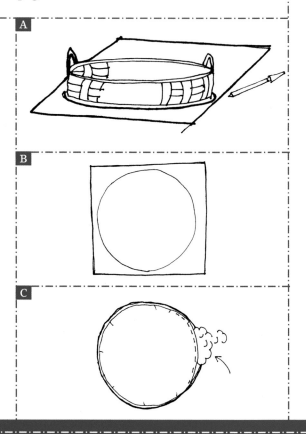

A

B

C

HINTS AND TIPS
- It's okay if the pillow is a bit too small; with the weight of a cat on it, it will fill the tray or basket in nicely. If it's too big, you can make the pillow cover a bit on the small side, and then the pillow will be smaller, too.
- This works with a basket that has a flat bottom. But don't feel limited to wicker; wood would be nice, too.

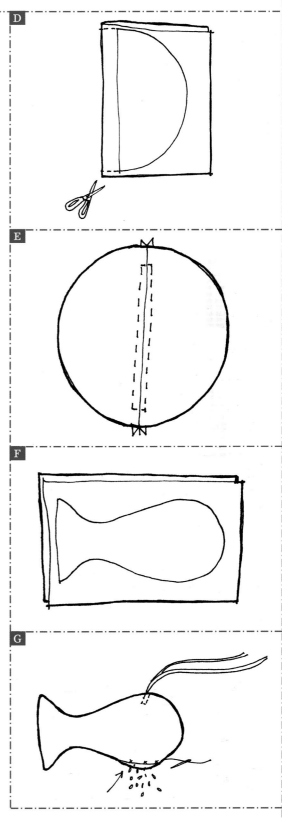

4. Insert zipper E (see The Basics, page 37). With the zipper opened halfway, place top and bottom fabrics right sides together. Stitch all the way around the pillow. Turn and insert the pillow form and zip up. Place in the basket.

5. Make the catnip fish by tracing the pattern onto the fabric. Sew on marked line through both pieces of fabric, right sides together, leaving an opening to turn. F

6. Turn and trim. Fill with catnip and then use a small part of a cotton ball or a bit of poly-fill over the catnip before you hand sew closed to keep the catnip from spilling out while you sew it shut. Hand or machine stitch a length of ribbon to the fish and tie it to the basket. G Find your cat and put it in there!

interiors: cool projects
you can live with

Clever Coasters

These coasters will keep your table from getting water rings and add a bit of sass to your interior accessories collection. Rubber stamps used on seam binding allow you to customize these, so have some fun!

MATERIALS FOR 4 COASTERS
Front and back fabric: (8) 5½" × 5½" (14 × 14cm) pieces
Facing: (4) 5½" × 5½" (14 × 14cm) pieces
Binding: (4) light-colored 6" (15cm) strips (One package will leave extra for mess-ups—and this is good.)
Alphabet rubber stamps, as small as you can find
Waterproof fabric pen, Pigma brush pen, or a fabric stamp pad

SEAM ALLOWANCE: ¼" (6mm)

1. Cut out all the pieces, including the strips of binding. On four of the binding strips, stamp the letters (see The Basics, page 47). Do this on each piece of tape; remember to make one of them say "mine." Heat set. **A**

2. Place rubber-stamped tape onto the top fabric and stitch along top and bottom of tape edge. Position so your letters are at least ⅜" (13mm) away from the coaster edge. **B**

3. Lay out the facing piece, then the back and front of the coaster, with right sides facing. Sew all the way around, leaving a small opening to turn inside out. Turn and press. **C**

4. Edge stitch, catching the opening closed while you sew. Press again. **D**

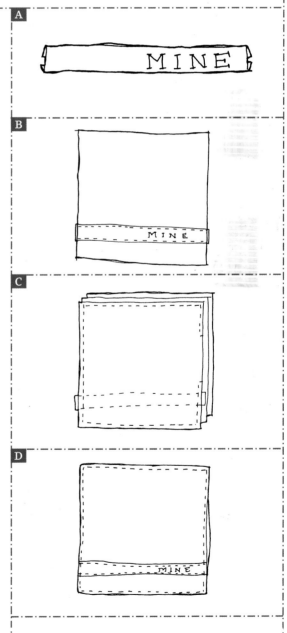

Mixy-Matchy Napkins

Get the paper towels off the table. You will never want to wipe your mouth with them again after you realize how simple it is to make these, and what a nice luxury they are! Start the day right with an espresso, a buttery croissant, and a lovely cloth napkin. These are all mixed and matched to help use up your extra fabrics from other projects, but a matching set would be lovely, too. Any size you like would work. These are a smaller luncheon size, but use whatever size feels right to you.

MATERIALS

Napkin fabric: (4) 14" × 10½" (35.5 × 26.5cm) pieces

SEAM ALLOWANCE: ⅜" (9.5mm)

1. Cut out the four pieces.

2. Hem the napkins. Do this by turning up and ironing a really small amount of fabric on two opposite edges. Don't burn yourself, but try to make the hem smaller than a ¼" (6mm). Then, at the machine while you sew, turn up another hem, about ⅛" (3mm), and stitch down. Pins get in the way here, so don't use them. **A**

3. Repeat with other two edges. **B**

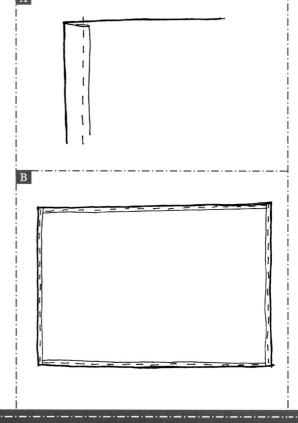

A

B

HINTS AND TIPS

- When sewing narrow hems, start sewing ½" (13mm) from the edge, backstitch, and then continue forward. Trying to start at the very tip can cause the fabric to jam up in your machine.

Tea Cozy

Teapots hold a special place in my heart, and so I feel they deserve clothes. I'm not alone in this opinion: tea cozies have been around a long time. This modern interpretation is lined with a flannel polka-dot print, keeping the pot extra warm.

MATERIALS

Outer fabric: (2) 12" × 12" (30.5 × 30.5cm) pieces of linen

Lining fabric: (2) 12" × 12" (30.5 × 30.5cm) pieces of cotton flannel

Bias trim: about 24" (61cm)

Ribbon for the top: about a 5" (12.5cm) piece

Embroidery floss or thick thread (optional)

Fabric paint or markers (optional)

Your favorite teapot as a fit-model

Freezer paper big enough for template

SEAM ALLOWANCE: ½" (13mm)

PATTERN AND TEMPLATE: pages 130 and 131

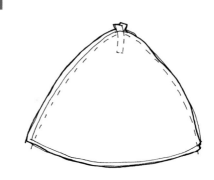

1. Cut out the pattern and, using masking tape to keep the sides together, place it over you favorite teapot to make sure it fits. Remember it will be even smaller when you sew it because of the ½" (13mm) seam allowances. If it is too small, redraw the pattern and adjust the template or enlarge on a copier. This was designed to fit a small teapot.

2. If you are painting and hand sewing on the linen, do that now. Trace the pattern shape onto the fabric front, but don't cut the piece out. Using the template, transfer the design (see The Basics, page 35) and paint. Let dry and heat set. Remove the freezer paper and hand stitch the template design using a running stitch and back stitch (see The Basics, page 45).

3. Cut out the fabric from the pattern. Cut a length of ribbon for the top of the cozy about 5" (12.5cm) long. Fold in half and pin in place with the folded edge of the ribbon facing down. Sew the outside front and back right sides together around sides and top only, catching the ribbon ends, leaving the bottom open. Turn and press. A

4. Sew the lining right sides together along the sides and top only. Turn and press.

5. Insert the lining into the outer fabric cozy. The wrong sides face together here, so it will look as if it is all done. The lining will be a bit longer; trim as necessary to make the bottom edge even.

6. Apply bias trim using the machine-and-hand method (see The Basics, page 40), machine stitching into place and then hand sewing the inside edge to the lining. B Turn under raw edge of binding at the end. Place on your teapot and hear her whisper "thank you."

HINTS AND TIPS

- Try changing the overall shape—a square, rectangle, or oval would be fun.

- I have used fabric paint and hand stitching on the linen, but this is optional. A great print is all you need to dress up your own little teapot.

Modern Table Runner

I designed this to showcase two vintage Vera napkins I had that were once my grand-mother's. This style of table runner can be any length or width, so measure your table first. The machine appliquéd circles can be placed in any random pattern that pleases you.

MATERIALS

The table runner shown is approximately 89" × 14" (2.26m × 35.5cm) and uses the following amounts of fabric (yours will vary depending on your window size).

Top fabric: (1) 90" × 15" (2.28m × 38cm) piece of linen (you may have to piece this, which is just fine)

Contrasting top fabric: (2) 16" × 12" (40.5 × 30.5cm) pieces (I used the vintage napkins here)

Back fabric: (1) 90" × 15" (2.28m × 38cm) piece of cotton flannel for the back

Scraps of contrasting solid fabrics for the circles (I used 3 colors): approximately 8" × 10" (20.5 × 25.5cm) of each color

SEAM ALLOWANCE: ½" (13mm)

1. Lay your vintage napkins (or contrasting rectangles of any other fabric) out on your table and determine the overall width. If you are changing the size of the example, add 1" (2.5cm) to your width and cut the front linen and back flannel fabric out. You will probably have to sew these together to get the full length. Try to do this in thirds, or at least avoid having one seam in the middle. A

2. Mark where the napkins look good and then sew them into the runner. B The drawing shows this better than words do. C

3. Now your top is done. Lay the top onto the flannel and with right sides together sew around top, bottom, and one side, leaving the other short end open for turning. D Turn inside out and press. Machine stitch open end closed, folding the raw edge in.

4. Stitch in the ditch around the napkins and the seams. E

5. Cut out the circles on your three contrasting fabrics and lay them out. You can copy the example here or do your own thing. Pin in place and machine appliqué (see The Basics, page 43). F

HINTS AND TIPS

- Old linen napkins can be really stretchy and hard to work with. This means there will be some puckering and tucks when you are all done, but that is part of the charm, so don't worry about it.

- This runner can be any size you want, and you don't have to have the runner hang off the table. Try making one for an entry table or even the top of a dresser.

- The subtle colors and natural palette make this runner look more modern. Stick with the natural colors if you like this look.

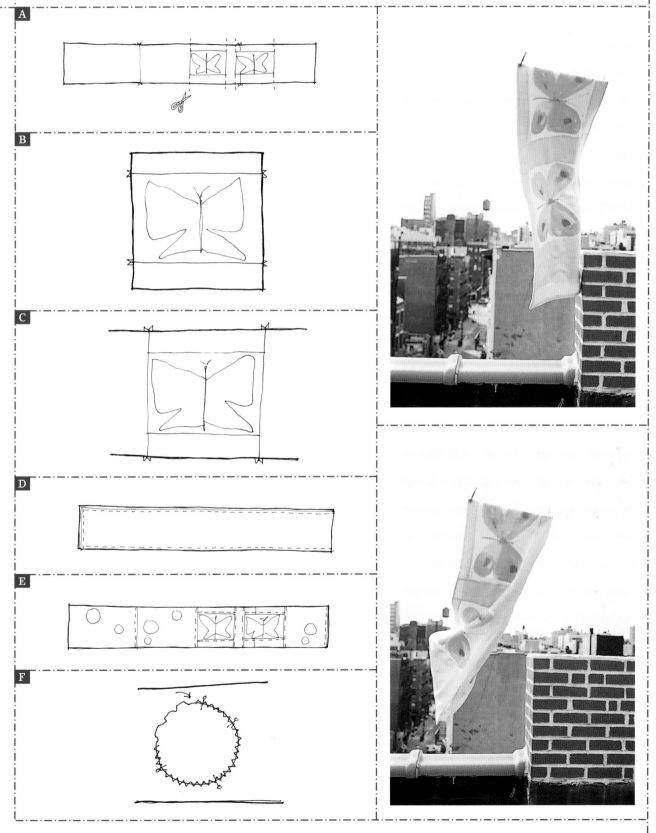

Place Mats

This simple place mat is trimmed with binding, but you can use ribbon or anything that has a finished edge. The contrasting fabric is top stitched down, and you only need a little. This is a perfect project for a small amount of fabric.

MATERIALS FOR 4 PLACE MATS
Top contrasting fabric: (4) 14$\frac{1}{2}$" × 10" (37 × 25.5cm) pieces
Front and back fabric: (8) 17" × 13" (43 × 33cm) pieces
Facing: (4) 17" × 13" (43 × 33cm) pieces
Ribbon or binding: 6$\frac{1}{2}$ yards (5.9m)

SEAM ALLOWANCE: $\frac{1}{2}$" (13mm)

1. Cut out all the pieces. On four of the place mat top pieces, lay out and center the four contrasting pieces. Pin. Sew around the edges with a basting stitch. A

2. Lay out the ribbon or binding, but do not cut. B You will use one continuous piece. Fold the miter at the corners and pin as you go. C Fold under the raw edge of the ribbon overlapping at the end. D Edge stitch on both sides of the ribbon. Go slowly and take out the pins as you stitch. E Press to make it flat and pretty.

3. Lay out the cotton flannel, then the place mat back and the place mat top with right sides facing. Stitch all the way around, leaving an opening to turn inside out. F

4. Turn inside out. Poke out the corners carefully so they don't become stretched out. Press. Edge stitch, catching the opening closed when you do this. Press again. G

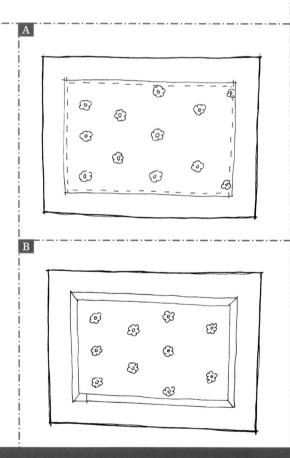

HINTS AND TIPS
- You can do more than one row of edge stitching. Try a contrasting color if you are feeling crazy.
- Skip the contrasting fabric and ribbon altogether for a really simple place mat. This would look great with a bold fabric pattern.
- Are your place mats slightly different sizes? Who cares! Lay them all out and pretend to set the table. You can't even tell, huh? You only notice size differences when you stack them and put them away, so don't sweat it.
- Add matching napkins for an amazing set. What a great wedding gift!

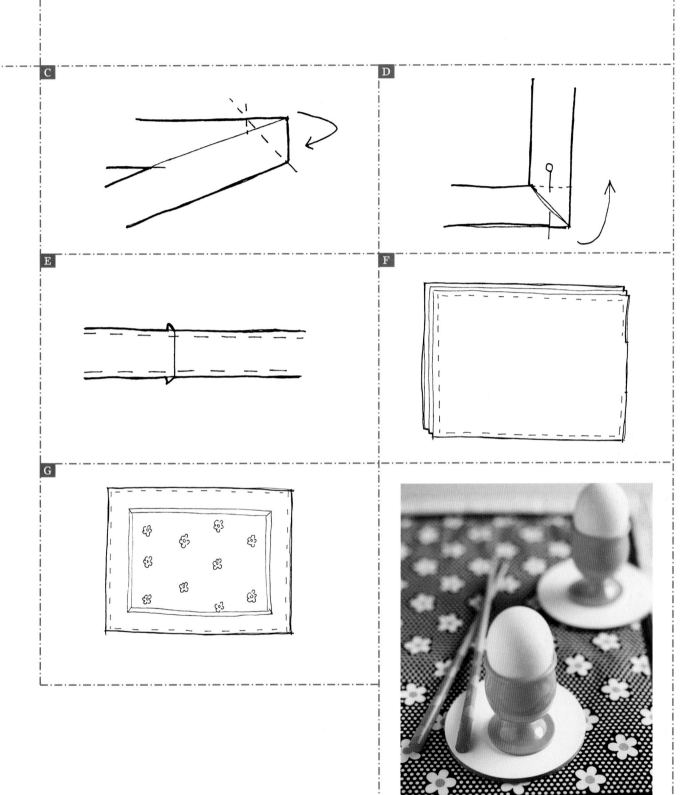

C

D

E

F

G

Easy Lap Quilt

This is the perfect project for a first quilt. All the basic techniques are in this quilt, but it's small and simplified, so you won't feel overwhelmed. It's strip-pieced together and the directions are pretty loose. You can do your own thing here, or copy the example exactly. Simple straight-line machine quilting makes it easy to get through your machine at home (no special walking foot needed) and then just add the binding. Easy!

MATERIALS

Quilt top: (3) solids ½ yard (46cm) each, cut into 5½" × 44" (14 × 111.5cm) strips
    (3) prints ¼ yard (23cm) each, cut into 5½" (14m) strips
Quilt back: (1) 44" × 44" (111.5 × 111.5cm) piece
Quilt batting: (1) 44" × 44" (111.5 × 111.5cm) piece
Quilt binding: Solid fabric with some pattern thrown in (included in above quantities) 2½" × roughly 4½ yards (3cm × 4.1m)

SEAM ALLOWANCES: ¼" (6mm)

FINISHED QUILT SIZE: approximately 40" × 40" (102 × 102cm)

1. Cut eight strips out of the solid fabric 5½" (14cm) wide and 44" (111.5cm) long. Now cut out strips of the patterned fabric 5½" (14cm) wide and vary the lengths. On the floor, lay out your solid stripes in the order that looks good to you. Then lay the patterned pieces on top of the solid strips, where they look good, trimming to the length you want them to be. (Remember they will be ½" [13mm] shorter with the seam allowance.)

2. When you are happy with the pattern, take a photo for easy reference. Now pin the patterned pieces where you have placed them and cut the solid fabric out behind them. With right sides together, sew the patterned pieces into the solid pieces, forming your strips. This method is a bit wasteful but the easiest if you are designing while you go, which is how I make quilts. A

3. When your strips are done, sew the rows together, with right sides facing. B Trim the edges when all the rows are together, making the quilt top as even as possible.

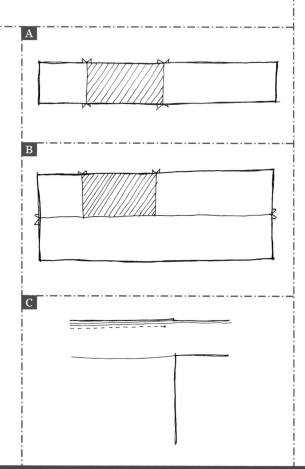

A

B

C

4. Sandwich your batting between your top and your backing fabric with right sides facing out. The batting and the backing should be about ½" (13mm) larger all the way around. Pin the top all over, work from the center out, and machine quilt (just use a normal straight stitch) all the seams between the strips—this is called "stitching in the ditch." Then add a few more straight seams in each strip at random intervals. A good rule is to have no more than 4"–6" (10–15cm) between quilted lines to keep the batting from shifting when washing.

5. Make the binding. Stitch the length together. You can add a few random patterned pieces in between the solid strips if you like. Sew the strips together until you have made enough binding. Then iron the strip in half lengthwise. Pin raw edges of the binding to quilt top edge and start to sew, but not in a corner. C

6. When you get to a corner, stop about ¼" (6mm) from the edge. C Then fold the strip straight up, making a diagonal line. D Fold straight back down over the fold you just made and resume stitching ¼" (6mm) from the edge. This will not look right until you turn and hand-stitch to the back, just trust me. E

7. Trim extra batting and backing even with the quilt top and wrap the fold edge of the binding over the quilt edge and onto the back, hand sewing down into place using the invisible hem stitch. When you get to the mitered corners, stitch up the diagonal line on both sides with a tiny slip stitch. F This binding will take some time, so do this while watching a movie, with the quilt on your lap. Congratulations—you've just made a quilt! G

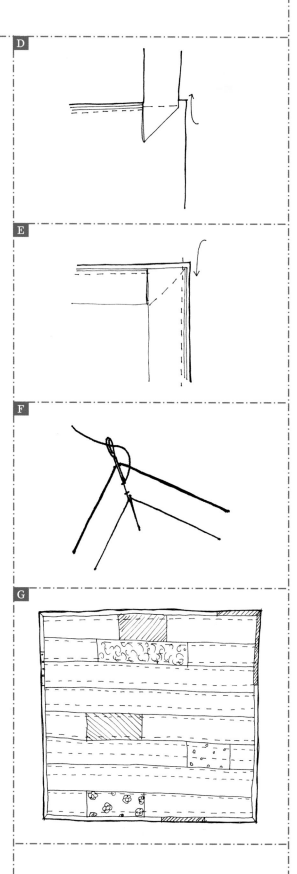

Pillows Three Ways

Here's a group of pillows for you. If you try all three types, you will know a lot about making pillows. The covered piping, ball fringe, and pleated ruffles are all available premade and ready to go. Just add some fabric and pillow inserts, and you have yourself some good-looking pillows. Change the shapes and sizes as you see fit. Pillows look better when they are socializing, so plan on making several.

MATERIALS
Variety of pillow forms
Fabric: Enough to cover your pillow insert, about the same size as the pillow, adding a couple inches. If you don't have a pillow insert yet, buy ½ yard (.45m) for each pillow. (This is a safe amount for most pillows; buy more if you are making large pillows.)
Trims: Ball fringe, fabric-covered cording, premade ruffles, buttons, etc. Buy enough trim to go around your pillow. It's best to just drape it around the pillow you are buying at the fabric store. Buy a bit extra just in case.

SEAM ALLOWANCE: ¼" (6mm)

SQUARE BALL-FRINGE PILLOW
1. The pillowcase should be about ½" (13mm) smaller than the pillow, so it will fill it out nicely and be plump. This means you should cut your square the same size as the pillow, or slightly larger. That gives you a ¼" (6mm) seam allowance. Cut two pieces. (Use the dimension of the pillow as stated on the label; don't actually measure the pillow itself.)

2. Cut a length of ball fringe needed to go all the way around and pin to right side of the front fabric with the balls facing in. Baste all the way around close to the edge; a zipper foot would be helpful here to get past the balls, but it's not necessary. A

3. Lay the other pillow piece on top, right sides together, and stitch all the way around, stitching inside the basting line. Leave a really big opening to turn. Turn inside out and insert the pillow.

4. Pin the opening closed and hand stitch with a slip stitch.

HINTS AND TIPS
- Using premade trims will help these pillows go together lickety split, but if you have time, try your hand at making your own trims. Polka dots and tiny stripes look supercute as ruffles.
- Because these cases are not removable, tuck the pillows away if things get rowdy.
- When making a pillow group, try to vary the fabric pattern scale for the best look.

Pillows Three Ways

SQUARE PILLOW RUFFLE WITH THE BUTTON TUFT

1. Roll ruffle edges onto themselves at the ends so there are no raw edges and stitch. Then stitch these ends together, slightly overlapping, making a continuous ruffle strip. B

2. Pin the ruffle to the right side of the front fabric facing in. Baste just on the inside of the finished edge of the ruffle, so when you turn inside out, only the ruffle shows, not the edge of the tape the ruffle is attached to. C Lay the ruffle on top of the bottom and—with right sides together—stitch, leaving an opening. Turn and press.

3. After inserting the pillow form and stitching closed, add the button tuft by sewing one button through with extra strong thread and then double knot on the other side, pulling tight. Sew a second button through and knot under the first button. This will indent the pillow, giving it the tufted look.

ROUND PILLOW WITH PIPING AND BUTTON TUFT

1. Cut out a circle, adding 1" (2.5cm) to the pillow form diameter.

2. Use the same steps as above but pin on the cording. To finish ends, cut off a bit of cording inside and then take out some stitches and overlap the cording, turning the raw edge under and making a continuous loop. D Baste to pillow with cording facing in. A zipper foot can help you stitch really close to the cording. E

3. Repeat step 3 above.

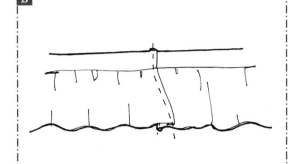

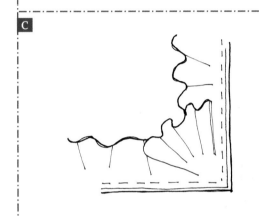

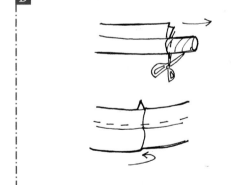

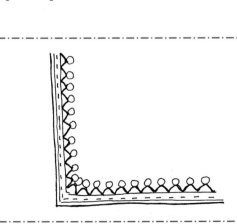

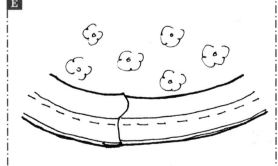

Semi-Simple Pillows

This wool pillow is a simple pillowcase pattern plus some fun. There is a contrasting fabric piece applied to the top, embellished with free-motion quilting and some easy hand sewing. If you want to keep it basic, just make the pillowcase. It's removable for easy cleaning and is my all-time favorite way to cover a pillow—quick, easy, and modern.

MATERIALS

18" × 18" (45.5 × 45.5cm) pillow insert
Front of pillow: (1) 18" × 18" (45.5 × 45.5cm) piece of wool (you can use cotton if you prefer)
Back: (2) 18" × 23" (45.5 × 58.5cm) pieces
Contrasting top fabric: 16" × 16" (40.5 × 40.5cm)
Embroidery floss

SEAM ALLOWANCE: ¼" (6mm)

1. Cut out all the pieces. The pillowcase is about ½" (13mm) smaller than the insert, so it makes a nice, plump pillow.

2. Free-motion quilt (see The Basics, page 41). **A** Sew around the various shapes and designs onto the contrasting top fabric. More is better with this technique, and it looks good sloppy, so don't worry about it. Add a hand-sewn running stitch with embroidery floss in areas where it will show up the best.

3. Turn under ¼" (6mm) on all four sides of the contrasting top fabric and press. Position onto pillow top fabric, facing out, and pin like crazy, working from the center out. Using a small zigzag stitch, sew all four edges down, stitching over the fabric edge. **B**

4. On the two back pieces, fold over ½" (13mm) on one short edge and press. Fold again and stitch. **C**

5. Make the pillow envelope. Lay out the embellished pillow top facing you. Then lay one piece of the back pillow fabric on top of that. Make sure the right side

HINTS AND TIPS

- The free-motion quilting with the hand-sewing detail is very forgiving and fun. It says, "Check me out—I am cool and artsy." Try it on handbags, place mats, and even curtains or existing clothing, or whatever else you can get your hands on.

of the hem is facing in. Then lay the other back piece down, with the hem overlapping the first, right side facing in. Pin all the way around, making sure to pin really well where the hems overlap. D

6. Stitch all the way around and turn it inside out. Press and insert the pillow form, punching and poking until it looks all nice and cozy.

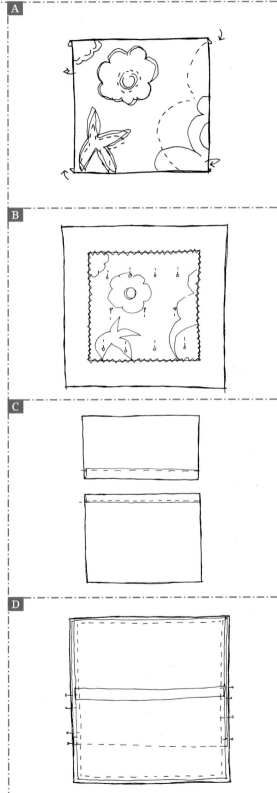

Painted Pillow Buddies

These pillows are your soft friends. You make your own pillow insert here, so you aren't limited to premade pillow shapes and sizes. I used soft-colored calicos on the front with a contrasting fabric on the back, but the sky is the limit. You can use the templates provided or just draw your own thing.

MATERIALS (FOR ONE PILLOW)
Front fabric: (1) 22" × 20" (56 × 51cm) piece
Back fabric: (1) 22" × 20" (56 × 51cm) piece
Cotton flannel facing: (2) 22" × 20" (56 × 51cm) pieces
Poly-fill loose stuffing
Fabric paint
Freezer paper big enough for template

TEMPLATES: pages 132–134

A

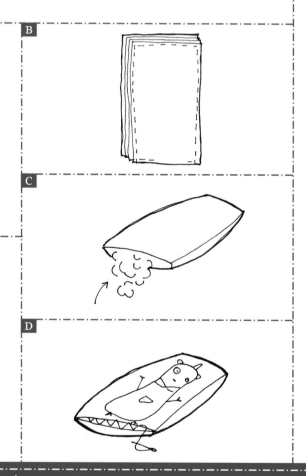

B

C

D

1. Enlarge template and transfer to front pillow fabric and outline the design with fabric paint (see The Basics, page 35). A Using the photo as a guide, embellish with a running stitch on pillow top.

2. Lay out both pieces of cotton flannel facings, and then the pillow front and back, right sides together. Sew around the marked outline. Leave a small opening at the bottom for stuffing. B Turn and press.

3. Stuff the pillow. C Pin closed and hand stitch with a slip stitch. D

HINTS AND TIPS

- These are really fun to make and seem to be happier in groups, so try making two or three together.

- This would be a great project for children. Have them either paint directly on the fabric or draw on paper first. Then a taller person can help enlarge and transfer the drawing onto the pillow.

Mistakes are always much
less noticeable in a week or so, and
in a month, the project will
look amazing.

Sugar-Sweet Curtains

These curtains are just the thing to give a room a bit of girly charm—perfect in a living room or bedroom where they can be hung over blinds or a roller shade, or just on their own. The split valance mimics a more traditional window treatment, looking as if you'd used a double rod, but it's all on one rod—very clever.

The valance piece is two pieces trimmed with a premade pleated ruffle and is attached to the simple solid color side panel. You can keep the side panels open with the ruffle tie back, or close them.

MATERIALS

The curtain shown is approximately 42" × 65" (106.5 × 165cm) and uses the following amounts of fabric for (2) panels and valances (yours will vary depending on your window size).

4 yards side panel fabric (54" [137cm] wide)
½ yard (.45m) valance fabric
3½ yards (3.2m) premade pleated ruffle
Velcro dots for tie-back
Small hook for tie-back (this goes into the wall)
One adjustable curtain rod that fits your window

SEAM ALLOWANCE: ¼" (6mm)

1. Measure the width and length of your window. **A** Remember to allow extra if the rod is hanging above the window frame. Cut the two long side panels. Each panel should be the width of your window, plus an extra 2" (5cm) to the width and about 5" (12.5cm) to the length. This will give you a nice full look.

2. Cut out the valance fabric the same width as the side panels. The height can vary depending on your window; the valance here is about 10" (25.5cm) high when hemmed. Hem the side of the two panels by turning up ½" (13mm), press and turn up another ½" (13mm) and top stitch. **B** Hem the bottom by turning up about ¼" (6mm) on the first turn and then about 1½" (3.8cm). Stitch. **C**

HINTS AND TIPS

- To make sure the panels turn out the same length, complete all the steps on both, checking for symmetry along the way. The last step will be attaching the valance and sewing the casing, so just go slowly here.

- The gathered look is very forgiving, so don't worry if the valances are slightly uneven. And if you tie back the curtains, you will never notice whether the side panel hems are slightly different lengths.

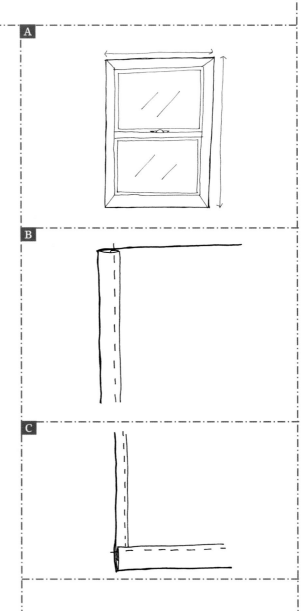

3. To make the valance, hem the sides as described in step 2. D For the bottom hem, turn up ½" (13mm) of the valance hem. Press. Turn up ½" (13mm) again and lay out the ruffle. Sew the premade pleated ruffle and the hem all at once. At the beginning and end, fold the ruffle onto itself so there are no raw edges. You don't have to pin this first, but make sure to cut way more ruffle than you think you need because it shrinks up when you attach it. E

4. Attach the valance to the panel at the top edge and then turn and press. F Stitch along the top through all layers to make the casing for the rod. G Make sure the casing is big enough to fit your rod before you do this. Repeat steps 2 through 4 for the other panel side. Install rod and hang.

5. If you want to make matching tie-backs, cut a length of ruffle and stitch edges closed at top. Stitch small snaps to edges. Install a small hook in the wall hidden behind the drapery. The tie-back hangs from the hook when the curtains are open. H

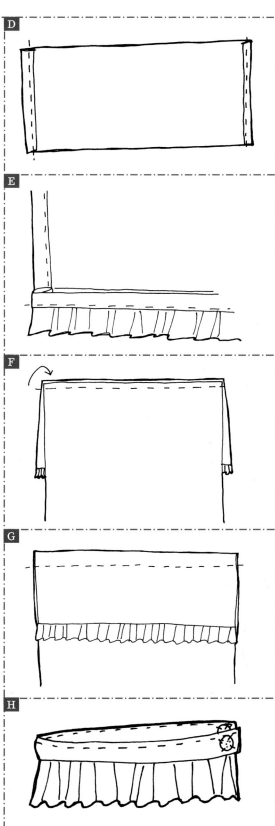

Café Curtains

Café curtains are wonderful because they allow a lot of light in while providing a bit of privacy—perfect in bathrooms and kitchens, where you don't ever need it to be completely dark. A valance with the exact same construction is added here, but you can leave that off if you prefer. Twill tape tabs require no finishing, so you can just sew them on. Grab a few tension rods, and you are done! The directions here are for the curtain shown. Make sure to adjust as necessary to fit your window.

MATERIALS FOR ONE CAFE CURTAIN AND MATCHING VALANCE FOR A WINDOW APPROXIMATELY 40" (102cm) WIDE

1½ yards (1.4m) curtain fabric (measurement based on 45"- [114.5cm-] wide fabric)
1½ yards (1.4m) of 2"- (5cm-) wide twill tape
Two tension rods to fit your window width—one for the valance and one for the curtain

SEAM ALLOWANCE: ¼" (6mm)

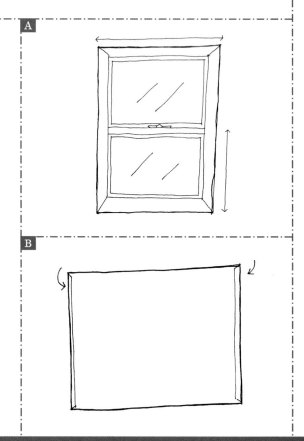

1. Measure the width and length of your window from the center to the bottom of the lower sill, where you want the curtain to end. If your window is really tall, you can just cover the bottom third with the curtain. A

2. Add 5" (12.5cm) to the overall length and 2" (5cm) to the overall width. Instead of cutting, make tiny cuts on the edge of the fabric and tear on the grain to get an even piece.

3. Turn over ½" (13mm) on the sides. B Iron and turn up another ½" (13mm) and stitch. C Do the same for the bottom hem, turning up a wider hem, about ¼" (6mm) on the first turn and then about 1½" (3.8cm) on the second. Stitch and press. D

4. Cut lengths of twill tape about 4" (10cm) and press in half. E Fold down top of curtain twice, just like the bottom hem, but before you edge stitch, pin the tabs in place, spaced evenly over the top hem. (I used five tabs for the 40"- [102cm-] wide window.) Before you sew down the hem and tabs, make sure the rod will slide through the tabs; adjust if necessary. Stitch two rows to make the hem, catching the tabs in both lines of stitching. F

HINTS AND TIPS

- A bold pattern can make this really simple design special. If you use a solid fabric, the stitching will show up quite a bit, so if you are nervous about it, use a patterned fabric. Make sure the fabric you use is lightweight enough. Hang it over the window to test it first and to see if enough light will shine through.

- Don't worry about the measurements too much. This is designed to be a bit roomy for the window, so there should be some subtle gathering. To be safe, err on the side of making the curtain too wide.

- You can keep this simple or go to town, adding ball fringe, ribbon, ruffles, or other trims. You can use this tab method to make full-length curtains as well—just make two panels for the window and adjust the width and length as necessary.

5. Repeat steps 2 through 4 for the valance—just make it shorter. This one is about 10" (25.5cm) high when hemmed.

6. Slide through the tension rod and hang. Looks great!

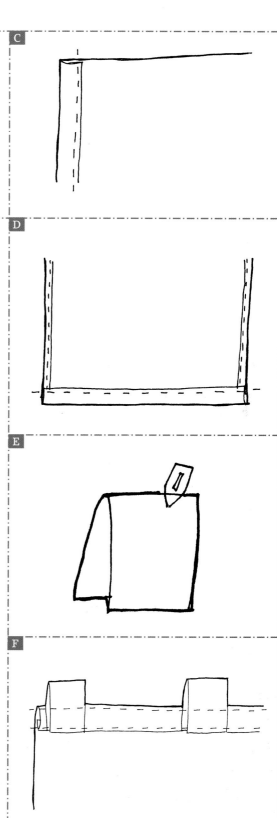

Amazing Tea Towel Apron

This project barely needs directions. You will never look at a tea towel the same way again. And tea towels really do make very good aprons. They are lightweight, absorbent, and perfect for getting down and dirty in the kitchen. Start your tea towel stash today!

MATERIALS

A tea towel. (We call them dish towels in our house, but tea towel sounds so much more refined.) Try using a vintage one if you are feeling extra cool. This will be worn with the long edge around your waist, so choose a pattern that won't look strange turned this way.

Twill tape: ½" (13mm) wide, or a bit wider if you like. About 4 yards (3.7m) per apron if you want the ties to wrap around the back and tie in front. You can also use grosgrain ribbon, or whatever else is soft enough to tie and make you happy.

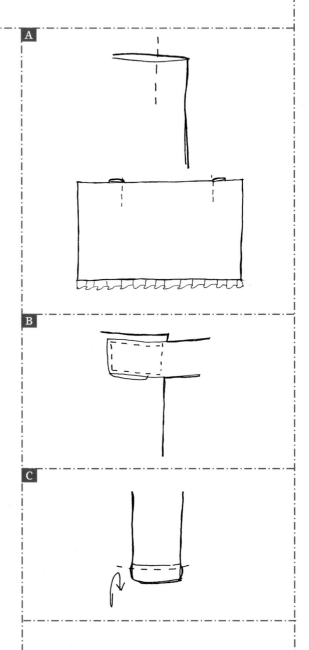

1. Add pleats on apron front if desired. To do this, pinch about 1" (2.4cm) of fabric onto itself 3" (7.6mm) from each side edge. Pin and stitch 3" (7.6mm) down from waist edge, creating the pleat. If you are adding a premade ruffle to the hem, do this now with a straight stitch. A

2. Cut ties from the twill tape for your apron. Fold one under and sew to the apron front. B Repeat on other side. Make your ties extra long if you want them to wrap around and tie in front. Turn the very end of twill tape under twice and sew down, covering raw edges. C

AMAZING APRONS

Aprons are a wonderful beginning sewing project and very dear to my heart. Here we have a modern tea towel apron, a basic vintage apron, and patterns for three types of pockets. Have fun with these and customize like crazy. These are addictive; you may even find yourself wearing one out of the house over jeans. How daring!

Being crafty is being creative, and creativity can be hard to handle sometimes. When you get in a rut and nothing is working out, or you feel uninspired, just relax and take a break. It's okay to have long periods of being "uncrafty." That's often when you can get the most inspiration,— when you aren't looking for it.

Vintage Apron

Here's a basic apron pattern that is the basis for almost every vintage apron I have in my enormous collection. Its gathered waist and flirty style is 100 percent retro. Lace, binding, contrasting hems, pockets, rick-rack, and embroidery can all be added to make your own vintage style. Try one of the apron pockets in this book or make up your own.

MATERIALS
Apron skirt: (1) 35" × 20" (89 × 51cm) piece
Apron waistband: (1) 24" × 4" (61 × 10cm) piece
Apron ties: (2) 27" × 4" (68.5 × 10cm) pieces (angle one end)
Trims and fabric for pockets: the sky is the limit

1. Hem the sides of the apron by folding over ¼"
   (6mm) and pressing. Turn again and stitch. Turn up
   bottom hem ¼" (6mm) and then 1" (2.5cm). Press
   and stitch bottom hem. Stitch ¼" (6mm) from top
   edge using a basting stitch. Gently pull on threads to
   gather. When gathered, top should be about 15"
   (38cm) wide. A

2. Fold ¼" (6mm) on all edges of the waistband, sides
   first and then the top and bottom. B

3. Lay gathered apron on the waistband folded edge
   and stitch. The right side of the apron should be
   facing you. C

4. Cut a diagonal line to make the end of the ties
   angled. Make a narrow hem on three sides by folding the edges over ⅛" (3mm) or so, and pressing.
   Turn again and stitch close to the edge. Do this on
   both ties, leaving one short end raw. Fold the short
   end to make it about 1½" (3.8cm) wide. Stitch close
   to edge. D

5. With the right side of the apron facing you, fold
   over the waistband and pin. Insert the tie ends into
   each waistband opening and stitch across the
   openings and across the length of the waistband
   bottom edge. E

   HINTS AND TIPS
   - Add pockets, trims, or extras before you gather
     the apron.
   - Try adding lace or binding the hem in a
     contrasting color.
   - Felt shapes are a quick way to embellish because you
     don't need to finish the edges.
   - Look at vintage aprons on eBay or in books to get
     ideas for finishing—it's amazing how many clever
     details are on these vintage aprons.

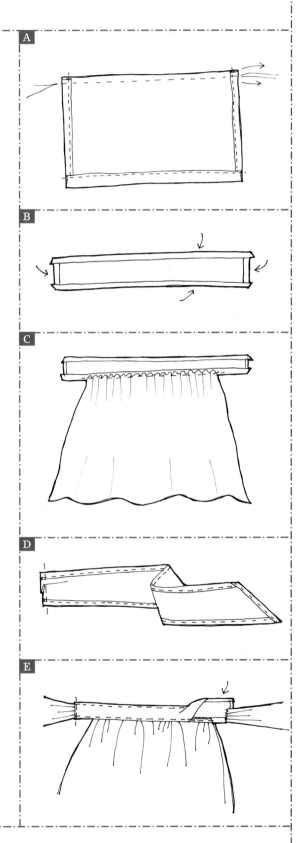

Apron Pockets

How can you have an apron without a pocket? Well, you can, but it's so much fun making the pocket that it's a shame to leave it off. It's a great way to use up little bits of fabric, and it gives you a reason to buy silly trims. Here are some pocket ideas. Once you make a few you will see how easy it is to invent your own.

MATERIALS
Pocket fabric: about an 8" × 8" (20.5 × 20.5cm) piece
Lining fabric, if needed: about an 8" × 8" (20.5 × 20.5cm) piece
Trims: ball fringe, felt, pleated ruffles, buttons, etc.

KANGAROO POCKET PATTERN, PAGE 134

1. Cut out the pieces from the pattern and sew right sides together, leaving a small opening. Turn and press. A, B

2. Edge stitch top diagonal pocket edges. Pin to tea towel front and stitch around top, bottom, and sides, leaving diagonal sides open for you hands. Tuck in the raw edges as you top stitch. C, D

3. Using a zipper foot, stitch the ball fringe down just under the pocket, turning under raw edges at the beginning and ending of the ball fringe. E

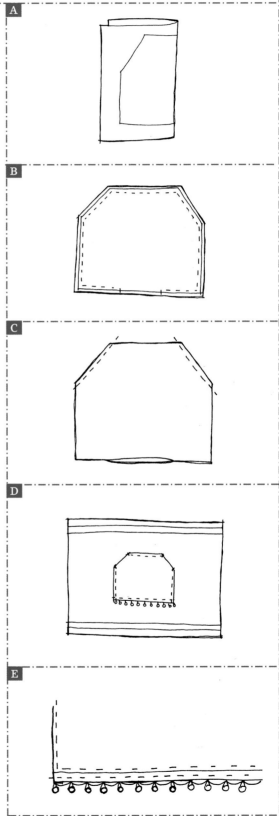

A

B

C

D

E

Apron Pockets

APPLE POCKET PATTERNS, PAGE 135

1. Cut out the pieces from the apple pattern A, and sew right sides together, leaving a small opening. Turn and press.

2. Cut out felt leaves using the pattern and sew onto apple front. Sew on the button. B, C

3. Place the apple on apron and pin. Using a zigzag stitch, sew around sides and lower edge, leaving the top open for your hand. D

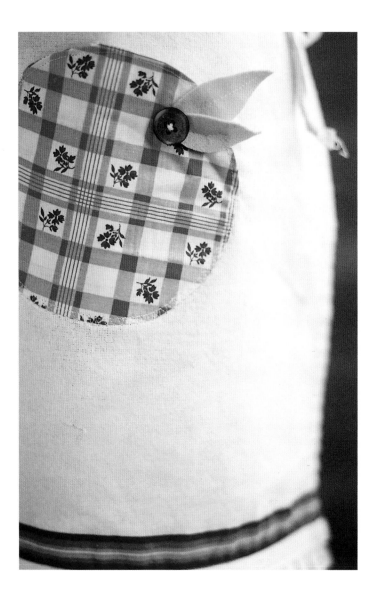

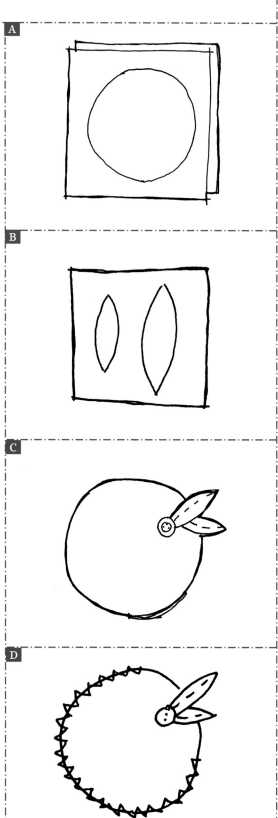

Apron Pockets

POCKET WITH BINDING PATTERN, PAGE 135

1. Cut out pocket shape. (I used two pieces for my pocket because they were small scraps. One piece works fine.)

2. Sew on binding with the zigzag method (see The Basics, page 40) on the sides and bottom of pocket. A Add binding across the top piece last, turning ends under. B

3. Pin to apron front and stitch on sides and bottom, just on the inside of the binding.

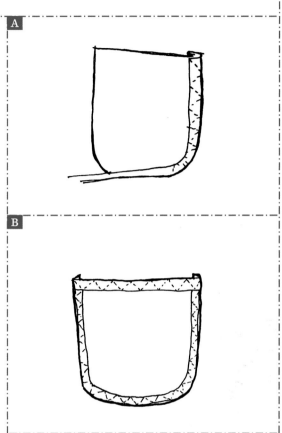

small people: for the special little person in your life

Woodland Elf Hat

It doesn't get any cuter than this. This wool hat keeps woodland creatures warm and toasty and puts a smile on everyone's face. The felt flower appliqué is embellished with a vintage button, but you can leave this off for your elf boys. Use an old sweater (felt it by washing and drying it first) like an unwanted merino wool sweater. You can also use a soft wool flannel from the fabric store. Wash and dry to felt before cutting out. This hat has raw edges on the inside, so use felted wool or other stretchy fabric that doesn't unravel.

MATERIALS
Felted wool: (1) 22" × 22" (51 × 56cm) rectangle
Felt flower: (2) small pieces of contrasting wool felt about 4" (10cm) square
Vintage button

SEAM ALLOWANCES: 3/8" (9.5mm)

PATTERN: page 136

1. If you are using a sweater, the ties can be cut from the arms, and the hat from the torso. If you are buying new wool for this, buy extra to allow for shrinkage, because it will shrink a lot when you wash and dry to felt it.

2. Lay out the pattern pieces, paying close attention to the grain direction as noted on the pattern. This is really important; otherwise, the hat won't stretch.

3. Starting from the bottom to the tip of the hat, sew together the two top pieces. A

4. Trim edges really close to the seam. Press flat. B

5. Sew the two back joined pieces together as shown C, then to either side of the hat top. Do this by pinning like crazy, easing the fabric around the curves. Stitch from bottom to tip of hat. Trim seams as above.

6. Trace flower shape from the template on the small contrasting felt, but don't cut out. Pin to hat and stitch inside the traced line of the drawn flower. Then trim using small scissors after it's sewn down, leaving about a 1/8" (3mm) edge. Cut out circle and sew on with button through all layers, knotting on inside of hat. D

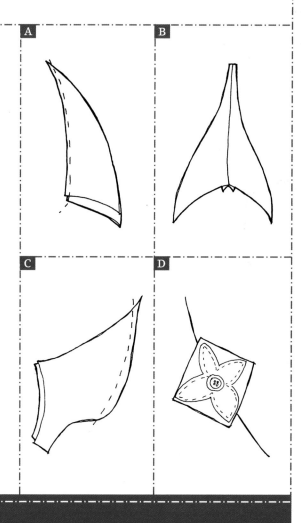

HINTS AND TIPS
- This hat is washable, but hang dry to avoid even more shrinkage.
- I prefer wool for these hats, but some people have wool allergies and some children can't stand wool. Cotton fleece is a great option because it's breathable and won't fray.
- You can experiment with the hat to make bigger sizes by cutting out the pattern pieces slightly bigger and longer, so as your children grow, they can still be elves.

Woodland Elf Hat

7. Make ties by folding two 1" × 14" (2.5 × 35.5cm) long strips of wool in half. Stitch across edge. E Trim close to edge. Tie a knot on one end. F

8. Turn ¼" (6mm) under all the way around the hat and edge stitch. It's easier to turn under while you stitch without pins. G Be careful to not stretch the wool while you do this.

9. Fold up hat ends ½" (13mm) toward inside. Lay unknotted tie end over and stitch through all layers. H

E

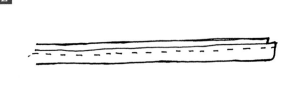

F

G

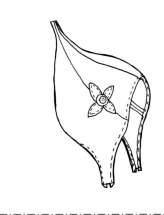

H

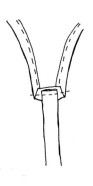

Many machines also can sew a variety of decorative stitches that are really fun and easy to use. Try adding some to your projects, but in small amounts. A little decorative stitching can go a long way, unless you are making something involved in yodeling.

Simple Bib

This is the best bib ever. It's cotton on the front and cotton flannel on the back. The snap makes it quick to get on (and hard for little ones to take off), and it's big enough for both messy eaters and drooly teethers. You can make it simple or have some fun with rubber stamps to make it extra special.

MATERIALS
Front fabric: (1) 12" × 10" (30.5 × 25.5cm) piece of cotton
Back: (1) 12" × 10" (30.5 × 25.5cm) piece of cotton flannel
Water-soluble pen (or other removable fabric marker)
Snaps (and a snap setter if you don't have one; they aren't expensive and are usually right next to the snaps in the fabric shop)
For rubber stamped variation:
Muslin or other solid fabric: roughly 1" × 2½" (2.5 × 6.5cm) (this will vary depending on the size of alphabet you use)
Rubber stamps
Fabric markers with a brush tip or a fabric stamp pad

PATTERN: page 137

1. Cut out pattern. On the flannel, trace the outline of the pattern with a removable marking method, marking where to leave the opening. Place the flannel on top of the front bib fabric, right side facing up. A Pin a few times and sew right on the marked line through both layers, leaving the space between the marks open.

2. Trim really close to the edge, about ⅛" (3mm) away, but leave about ¼" (6mm) where the opening is. B Turn inside out, using a chopstick or the eraser end of a pencil to help with the tight spots. Press. Top stitch all the way around the bib, going slowly around tight corners and catching the opening closed while you do this. Set the snap using the snap setter directions.

3. To add a rubber stamp label, cut out muslin and iron freezer paper on the back. Stamp away using the fabric marker to ink it (see The Basics, page 47) or a stamp pad especially made for fabric. C When you are happy with how it looks, iron ¼" (6mm) up on all four sides and pin to front of bib. D Using a zigzag stitch, sew all the way around the label, sewing slightly over the edge. Press.

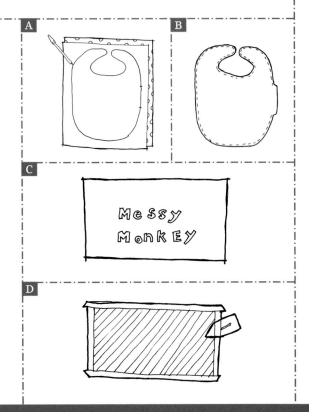

HINTS AND TIPS

- You don't need to use letters. Use any kind of rubber stamp. (Or be extra cool and carve your own!) Line art works better than large areas of color when using the fabric markers to ink the stamps.

- Stamping on muslin first gives you the ability to get it perfect before you sew it on, which means no ruining finished bibs.

- These are really simple to make assembly-line style. Try sewing seven, one for each day of the week. This would be a lovely shower gift. Also, try using "un-baby" looking fabrics—they will really stand out from what we are all used to seeing in the baby stores.

- These will get filthy! To wash, just throw them in the washing machine with the clothes, or, if they aren't really dirty and gross, just rinse them in the sink and wring them out, letting them air dry snapped to the highchair. They will dry overnight.

Scalloped Baby Blanket

This is a perfect shower gift that you can start and finish in one sitting. Okay, maybe one long sitting. Two lovely fabrics are sewn together with a scalloped edge and a cozy layer of cotton flannel in between. It's perfect as a bunting or swaddle blanket. Simple straight-line quilting through all layers keeps it from shifting.

MATERIALS
Quilt top fabric: (1) 30" × 34" (76 × 86cm) piece
Quilt back fabric: (1) 30" × 34" (76 × 86cm) piece
Cotton flannel for the inside: (1) 30" × 34" (76 × 86cm) piece

TEMPLATE: page 137

1. Cut out rectangles of all three fabrics.

2. On the back of the quilt top fabric, using a water-soluble pen, trace the template to make scalloped edge. A

3. Sandwich your quilt together with the cotton flannel down first, then the back and the top right sides together, so the scallop markings are facing you. You will stitch on this line. A

4. Pin from the center out to avoid shifting and follow the scalloped line with a straight stitch, pivoting at the scallops' inside points. Stitch around all four sides, leaving two full scallops open for turning.

5. Trim and notch around the scallops, leaving about a ⅛" (3mm) edge and snip at scallop inside points really close to the stitching. B Turn inside out and iron all the scallops out. Use your finger to help ease these out. Press.

HINTS AND TIPS
- There will be some shifting that occurs when you machine stitch this no matter how much you pin. Don't sweat it. If you use unwashed fabrics and then wash and dry this whole quilt after you complete it, it will shrink up, and the tucks will be less noticeable and add a lovely, shabby vintage charm to this blanket. Also, using a highly patterned fabric will help hide unwanted tucks and puckers.

- Because this blanket is so simple and is just two pieces of fabric and a lining, it's perfect for your favorite fabric that wouldn't get noticed in small pieces. A novelty print, an alphabet, or large graphic fabrics are perfect for the project.

- Cotton flannel would be a nice choice on one side of the blanket for extra coziness. If you want to use flannel on both sides, you can skip the flannel lining.

6. For the machine quilting, mark the quilt into thirds (or more lines if you prefer) in both directions, ideally between the scallops. Quilt through all layers with a straight stitch. C

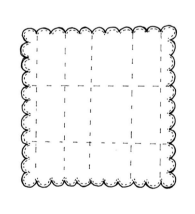

7. Edge stitch around the scallops carefully, tucking in raw edges on the open scallops. D Wash and dry before using.

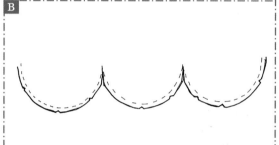

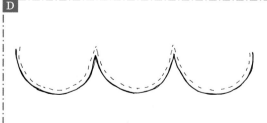

Soft Turtle Buddy

This corduroy and cotton turtle buddy is sad and needs a special home. The four legs are perfect for small fingers to hold onto. This stuffed toy project has several steps. They aren't hard, but go slowly for the best results.

MATERIALS

Turtle shell fabric: (1) 8" × 10" (20.5 × 25.5cm) piece
Legs, head, and tail fabric: (2) 8" × 10" (20.5 × 25.5cm) pieces
Contrasting felt for eyes
Poly-fill stuffing
Embroidery floss for eyes

SEAM ALLOWANCE: ¼" (6mm)

PATTERN: page 138

1. Trace patterns. A Cut out the top and two bottom shell pieces. Sew up the six darts on shell top. B, C

2. Trace leg, head, and tail patterns onto rectangles of fabric. Sewing through two layers of fabric, stitch on marking line, trim, and turn. D Do this for all four legs and the tail. Stuff with poly-fill and baste closed. E

3. Sew two head top pieces together, right sides facing. F Sew to the head bottom. G Trim, turn, and stuff with poly-fill. Baste closed.

4. Stitch two bottom pieces together, leaving open between marks. H

5. Pin head, legs, and tail facing inward on the right side of shell top. Baste around top edge, catching all these pieces. Now pin this top to the bottom shell, right sides facing. Stitch all the way around. I Turn though the opening in the shell bottom and stuff with poly-fill. Hand sew center opening closed. J

6. Cut small circles of contrasting felt and hand sew to head (see The Basics, page 45, on how to hide the tails and have a knotless start). K Finish the pupils with a French knot (see The Basics, page 45). L Now give your new buddy to a special friend.

HINTS AND TIPS
- Making soft toys is great fun. If you find running these small pieces through you machine a challenge, try hand sewing using a back stitch. You will have much more control.

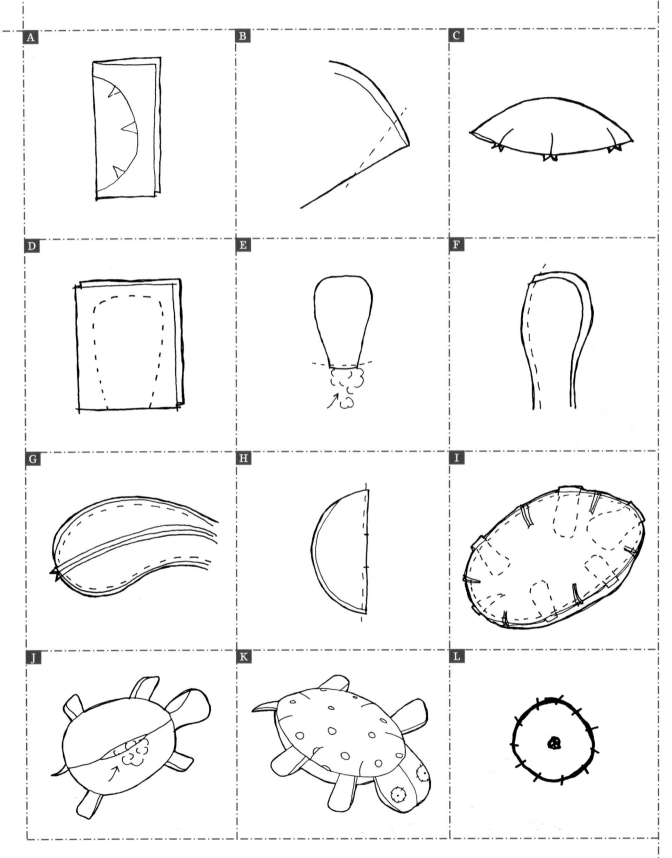

Puppet Theater
with a Matching Case

This is your answer for a rainy day. A simple tension rod hangs this puppet theater from any doorway. All you need are some puppets and an audience. The opening is trimmed with bias tape and curtains that tie open. Wood dowels are inserted in casings in the back to keep it straight, and it all rolls up and fits into its own matching storage case when the show is over.

This is not a hard project, but there are a lot of straight seams. It can get a little boring. Put on some good music and plan on doing this over a few days so you don't get burned out.

MATERIALS (TO FIT A 33"–34" [81 X 86cm] WIDE DOOR)
Fabric quantities:
  Plain pink: 2½ yards (2.3m)
  Floral: 1½ yards (1.4m)
  Green: 1 yard (1m)
Cut size for pink fabric:
  Curtain background: (1) 34" × 70" (86 × 177.5cm) piece
Cut sizes for floral fabric:
  Valances: (2) 34" × 15" (86 × 38cm) pieces
  Case: (1) 15" × 36" (38 × 91.5cm) piece
Cut sizes for green fabric:
  Curtains: (2) 13" × 25" (33 x 63.5cm) pieces
  Case flap: (1) 7½" × 14" (19 x 35.5cm) piece

NOTIONS
3 yards (2.7m) of ¼" (6mm) double-wide bias tape
Ribbon for tie-backs, 42" (1m) cut in half
2 yards (1.8m) of 2" (5cm) wide twill tape
(2) ½" (13mm) diameter wood dowels 32" (81cm) long
  (you may have to trim these with a saw)
2 yards (1.8m) ball fringe
Big button
Tension rod to fit doorway

1. Sew the side hems on the pink background by turning up ¼" (6mm) and pressing, and then another ¼" (6mm) and stitching. A Repeat for bottom hem, but turn 1" (2.5cm) on the second turn and stitch. B For the top hem, make the second fold 2" (5cm) (this will be where you insert the tension rod).

2. Make both valances by hemming the sides the same as above. Iron the top and bottom edges ¼" (6mm). C Sew ball fringe to bottom folded edge on the wrong side. D Repeat with other valance. Leave the top edge of the valance folded, but unstitched for now.

3. Fold pink background in half lengthwise, and mark the theater opening lightly in pencil. The marks should be about 15" (38cm) from the hemmed top edge and 6" (15cm) from the hemmed side edge, with the opening itself measuring about 14" (35.5cm) high. Cut out the opening on the fold. This may seem scary, but just draw lines to follow and round the corners. E Apply the bias trim to the opening. You can use a straight stitch and sew both sides at once; the tape is wide enough that this works fine. Fold over raw edge before ending the seam. F Start the tape in one of the upper corners where the overlapped seam will be hidden by the green curtain.

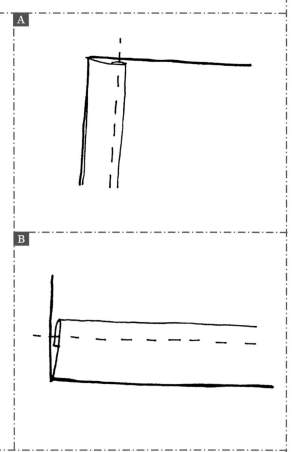

A

B

4. Stitch the two lengths of twill tape about ½" (13mm) above and below opening. Keep ends open. G This is where you will insert the wood dowels for stability. The seams will be concealed in the front by the valances.

5. Stitch both pieces of ribbon on the binding tape edge to make the curtain tie-backs. H

6. Hem the green curtains by folding and stitching the edges and hem as in step 1. Repeat for other curtain. I Place over the opening and stitch across top, positioning them ¼" (6mm) above the opening. J

7. Sew on valances. Stitch the top valance approximately 4" (10cm) from the top edge. Stitch the bottom valance along the bound opening, just below the twill tape seam. K

8. Lay the case piece out and fold in half lengthwise, right sides together. Stitch the side and bottom seam of the case together. L Fold the top down ¼" (6mm) and press, then turn again and stitch around opening. Turn right side out and press.

9. Fold the case top in half short-wise. Stitch sides. Turn. Fold under ¼" (6mm) of raw edge. Press. Top stitch around all sides. Make a buttonhole to fit your button. M

10. Stitch the case flap to the outside of the case back. Before you sew on the button, roll up the curtain with the dowels and rod inserted, and place it into your bag. Close the flap over and mark the button placement. Take everything out and sew on the button. N Now grab some puppets!

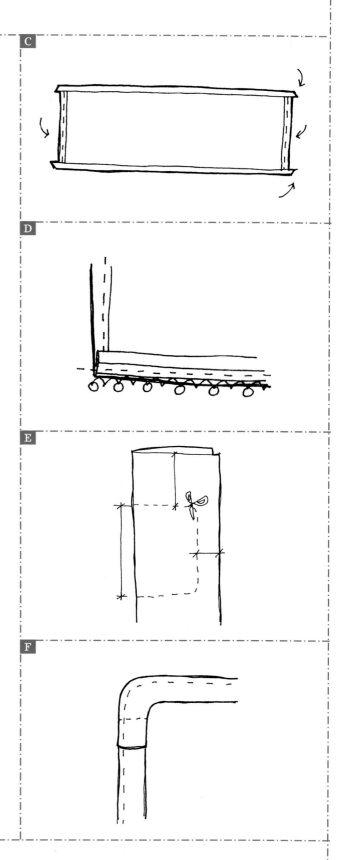

Puppet Theater with a Matching Case

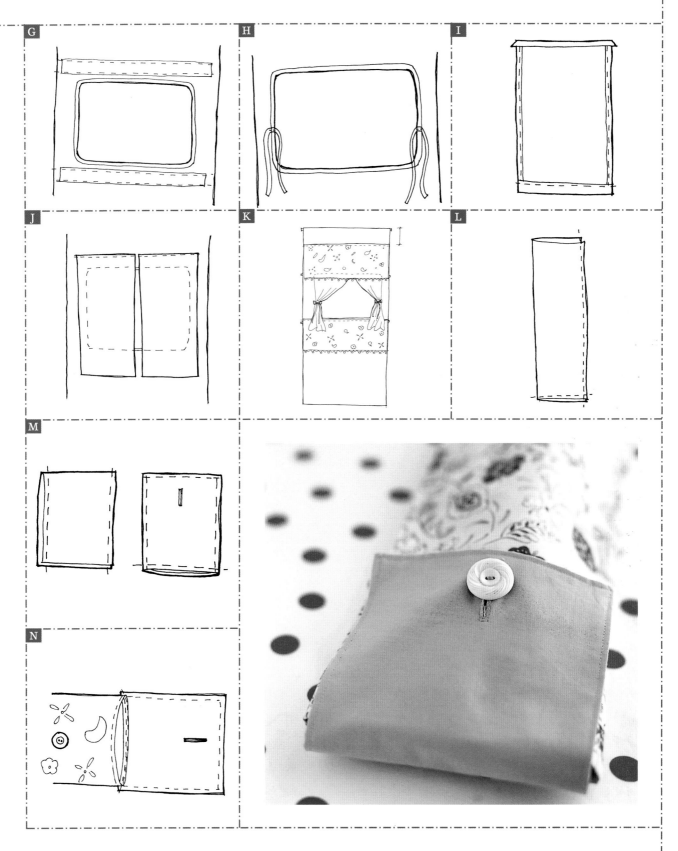

Sweet Wee Jacket

This one-piece jacket (18–24 months) is made with just two seams and is so easy you will think it's some kind of magic trick! It's finished with a bias binding at the neck that also acts as the tie. The unfinished raw edges on the turned up cuffs and hem give this jacket a sweet deconstructed look while making it even easier for you to sew.

MATERIALS
Fabric for jacket: (1) 36" × 24" (91 × 61cm) piece
    I used an organic cotton jersey, but a nonraveling fleece would work as well.
(1) pack of bias binding: ⅛" × ¼" (3 × 6mm) wide

SEAM ALLOWANCE: ⅜" (9.5mm)

PATTERN: page 139

1. Cut out pattern on folds. Pay close attention to the pattern notes; this needs to be placed to two folds so that the rectangle is folded in quarters before you cut. A

2. Sew underarm seams, right sides together. B Even up cuffs by trimming if necessary and then turn up. Cut up center of jacket (front only). Stay stitch around neck opening about ⅛" (3mm) from edge so the collar won't stretch when applying the binding.

3. Apply binding, leaving long tails on each end to tie. Apply the binding by machine and by hand (see The Basics, page 40), machine stitching on outside and hand sewing down on the inside. Machine straight stitch down both sides of ties to keep binding from unfolding. C You are done—can you believe how easy that was?

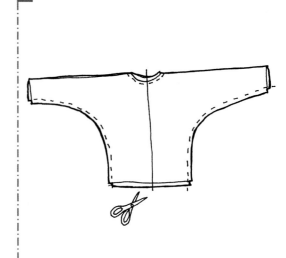

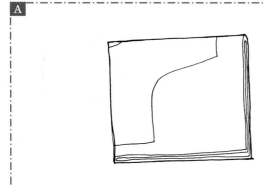

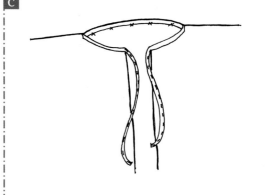

HINTS AND TIPS
- This jacket can be scaled down for a smaller child—just shorten the sleeves and the length. It's meant to fit loose, so its shape is forgiving, making it the perfect gift for babies to grow into.
- You can customize this jacket with buttons, pockets, and other trims.
- This pattern requires a really soft fabric that can drape, or else it will be too stiff to be comfortable.

My grandmother used to always tell my mom, "You have to be good enough to know when you can bend the rules."

Swing Swing Smock

This smock is just the thing to make your small people feel special—pretty enough to wear out and practical enough to wear while making a mess. The easy one-piece smock has just two seams at the shoulders, making this a perfect beginning project and the hit gift of any child's birthday party.

MATERIALS

Smock fabric: (1) 20" × 30" (51 × 76cm) piece
One pack of bias trim: about 4 yards (3.7m)
    I use the narrowest trim (⅛" [3mm] when folded in half) for this smock, but a larger width would look fine, too.
Contrasting pocket fabric: About a 5" × 5" (12.5 × 12.5cm) square

SEAM ALLOWANCE: ⅜" (9.5mm)

PATTERN: page 140

1. Using the pattern, cut out smock on fold of fabric. Cut out pocket as well. A

2. Sew up shoulder seams with right sides facing each other. Turn and press. B

3. Iron top down on pocket and top stitch. Iron remaining three edges of pocket and pin pocket in place as desired. Stitch on three sides of pocket, leaving the top open. C, D

4. Apply binding around armholes, sides, and bottom of smock using the zigzag method (see The Basics, page 40). E

5. Leaving a 15" (38cm) tail on each end (this extra length will make the ties), attach binding to neck. Zigzag on the tails to complete the ties. F

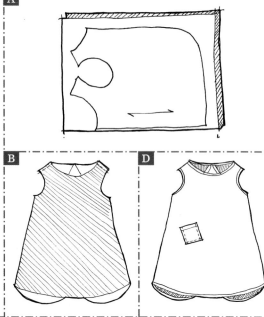

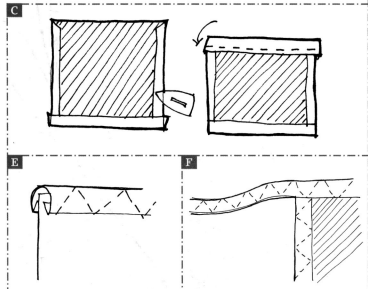

HINTS AND TIPS

- This pattern is roomy, so for older children you can just lengthen the original pattern.

- The pocket can be placed anywhere, and two pockets would look supersweet.

- For a hot summer's day, this pattern makes a lovely dress paired with bloomers.

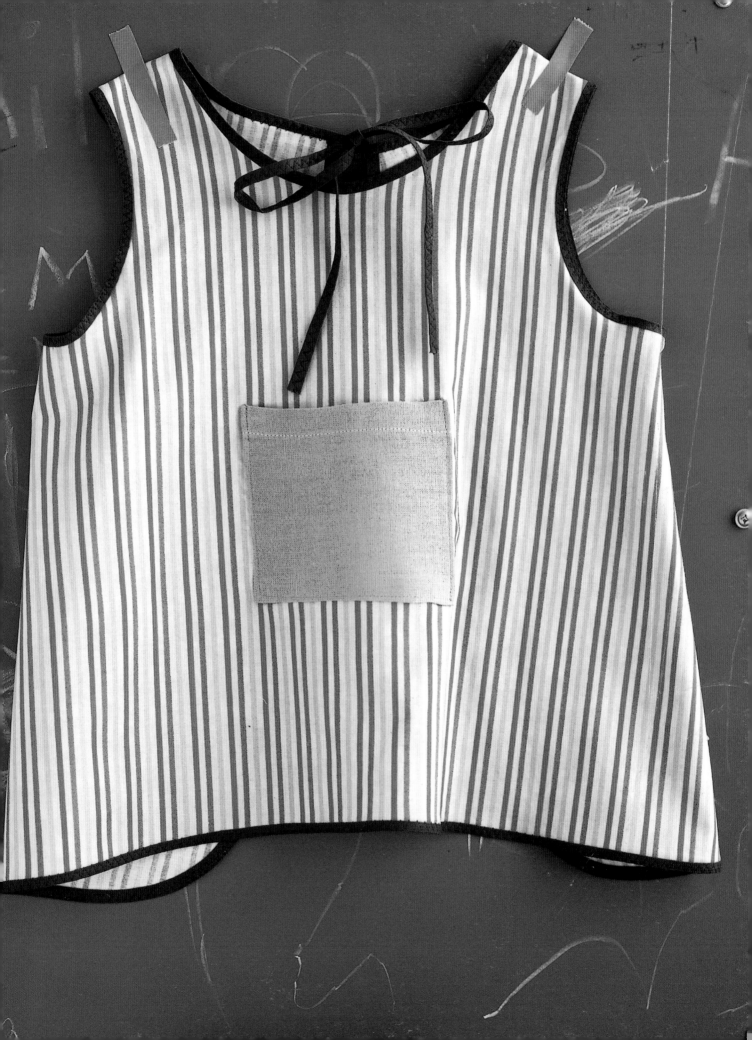

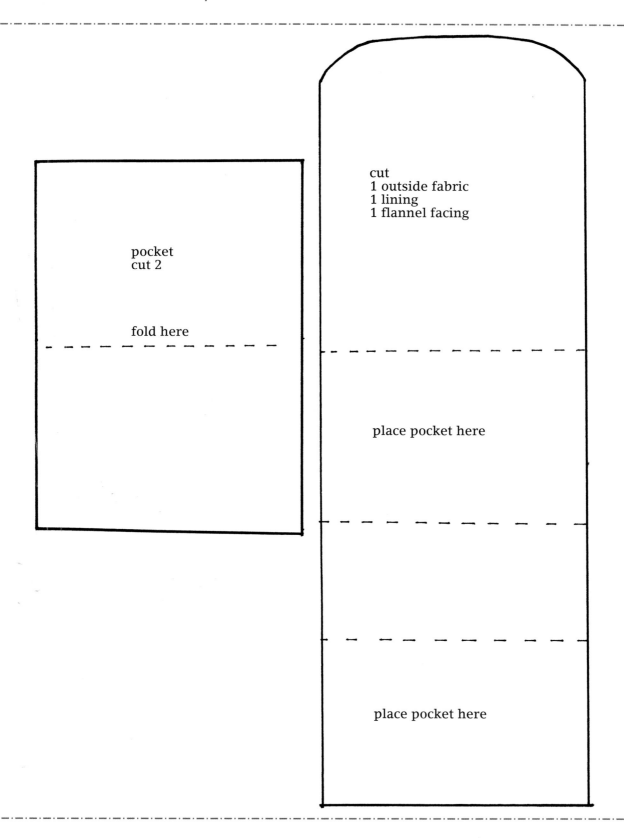

pocket
cut 2

fold here

cut
1 outside fabric
1 lining
1 flannel facing

place pocket here

place pocket here

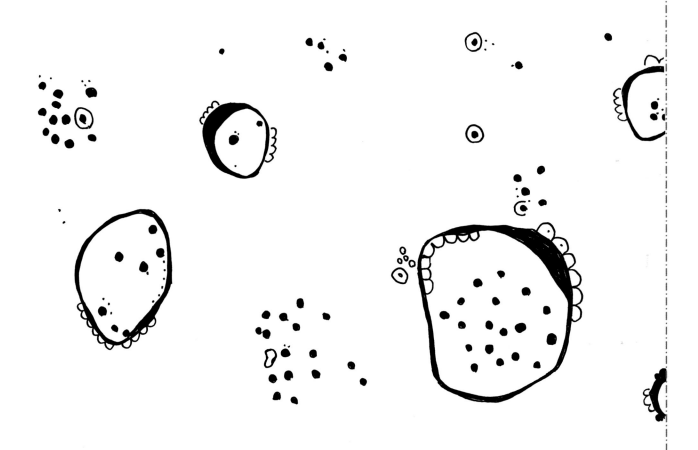

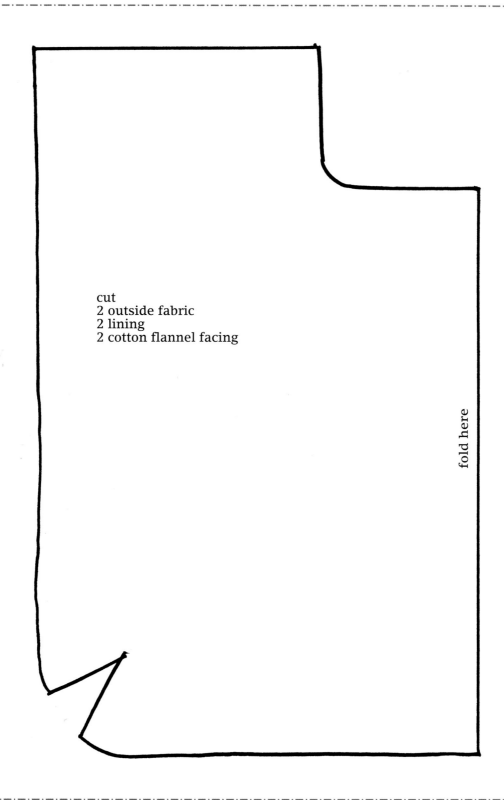

cut
2 outside fabric
2 lining
2 cotton flannel facing

fold here

cat tuffet in a basket | page 74 | use at 100%

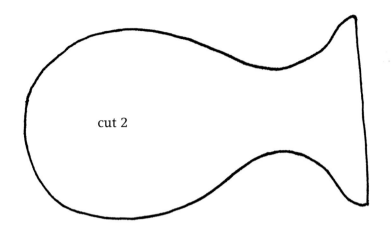

cut 2

tea cozy | page 80 | enlarge 200%

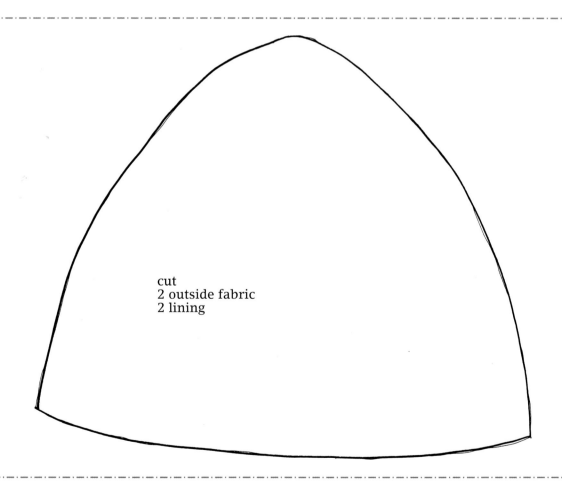

cut
2 outside fabric
2 lining

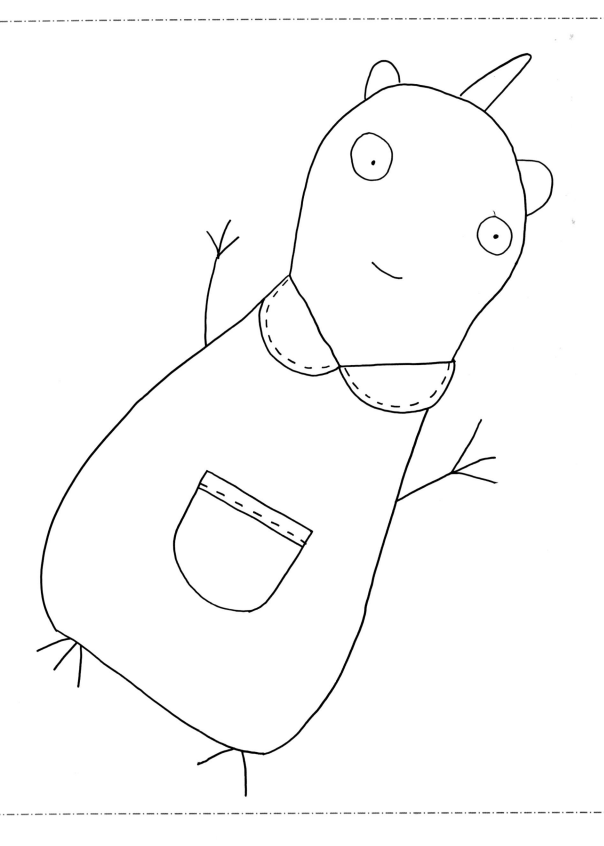

painted pillow buddies | page 94 | enlarge 261%

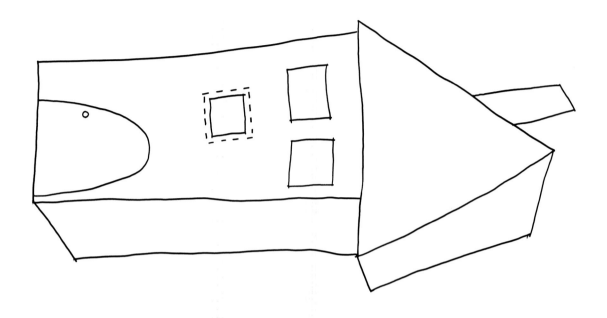

kangaroo pocket | page 105 | enlarge 200%

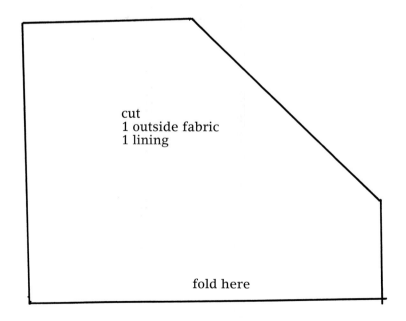

cut
1 outside fabric
1 lining

fold here

apple pocket | page 106 | enlarge 200%

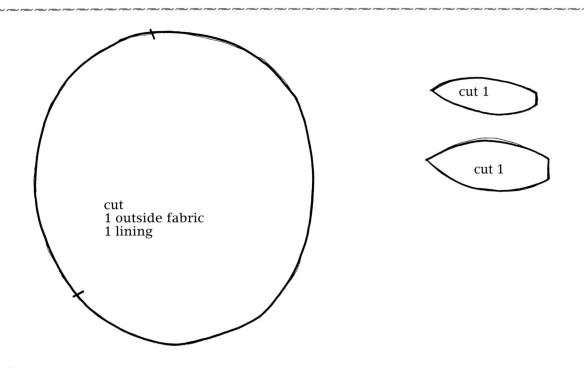

cut 1

cut 1

cut
1 outside fabric
1 lining

pocket with binding | page 107 | use at 100%

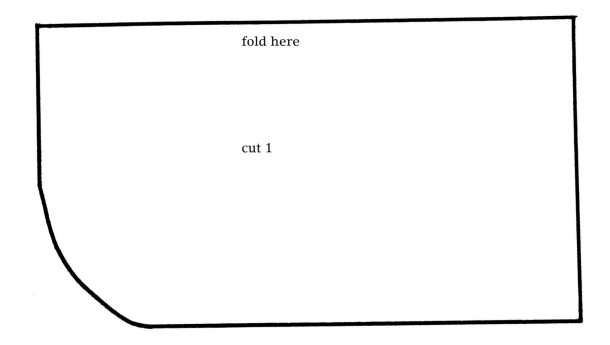

fold here

cut 1

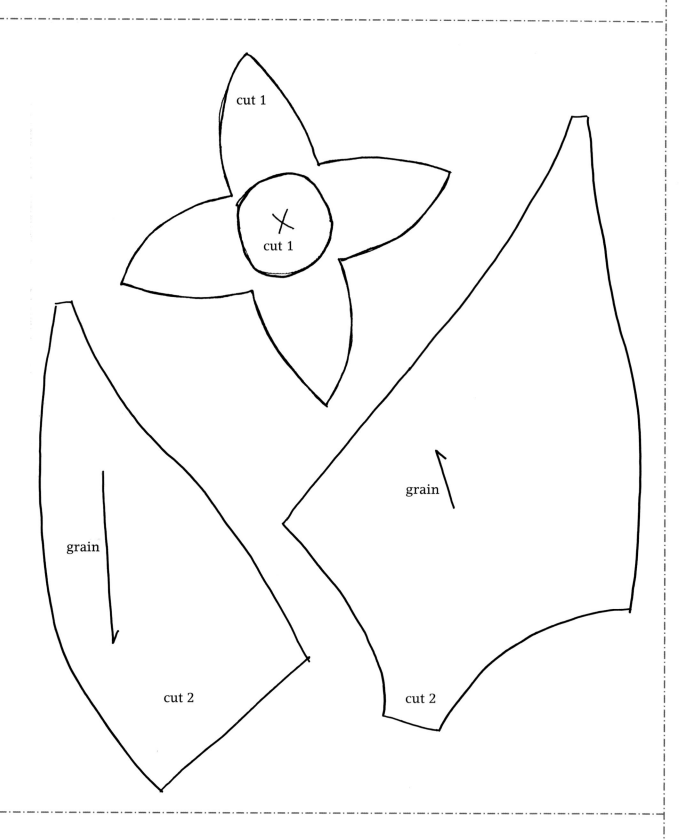

simple bib | page 112 | enlarge 175%

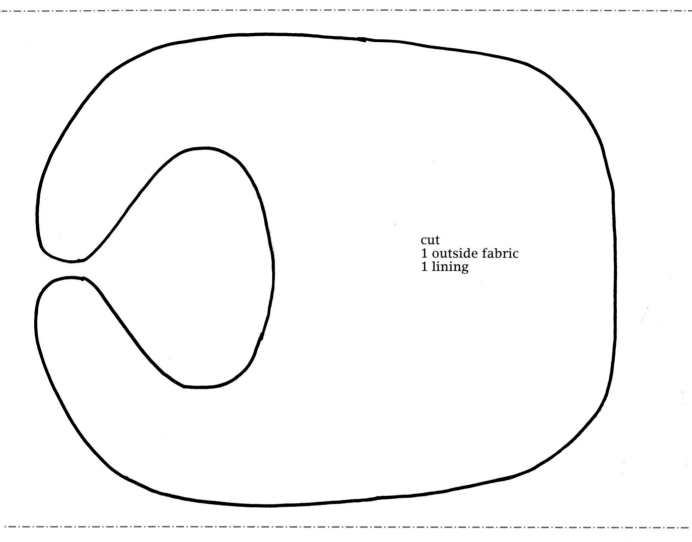

cut
1 outside fabric
1 lining

scalloped baby blanket | page 114 | enlarge 200%

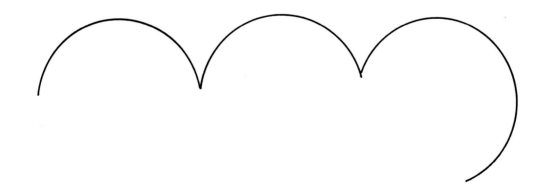

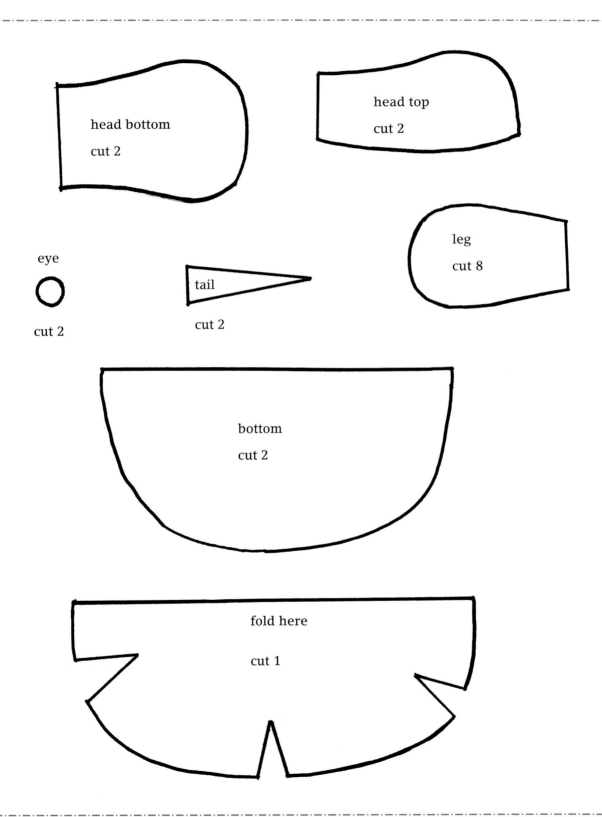

head bottom

cut 2

head top

cut 2

leg

cut 8

eye

cut 2

tail

cut 2

bottom

cut 2

fold here

cut 1

sweet wee jacket | page 122 | enlarge 215%

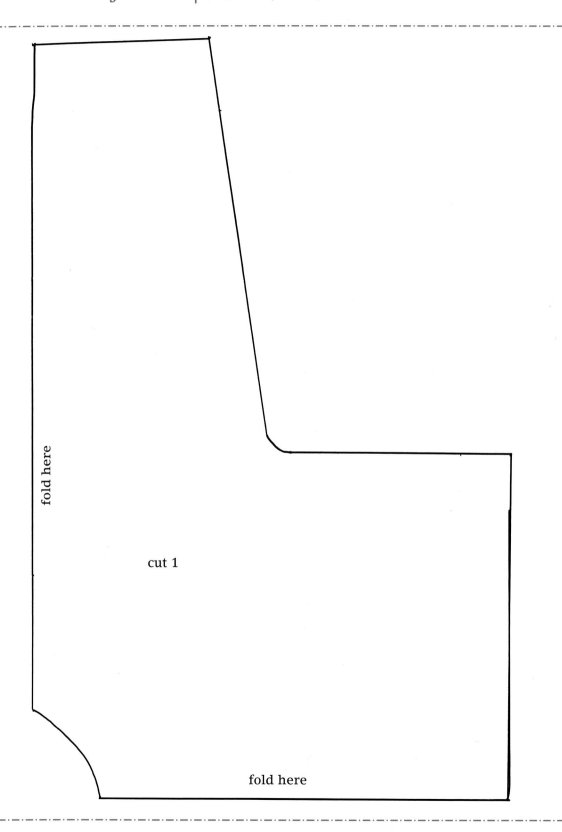

fold here

cut 1

fold here

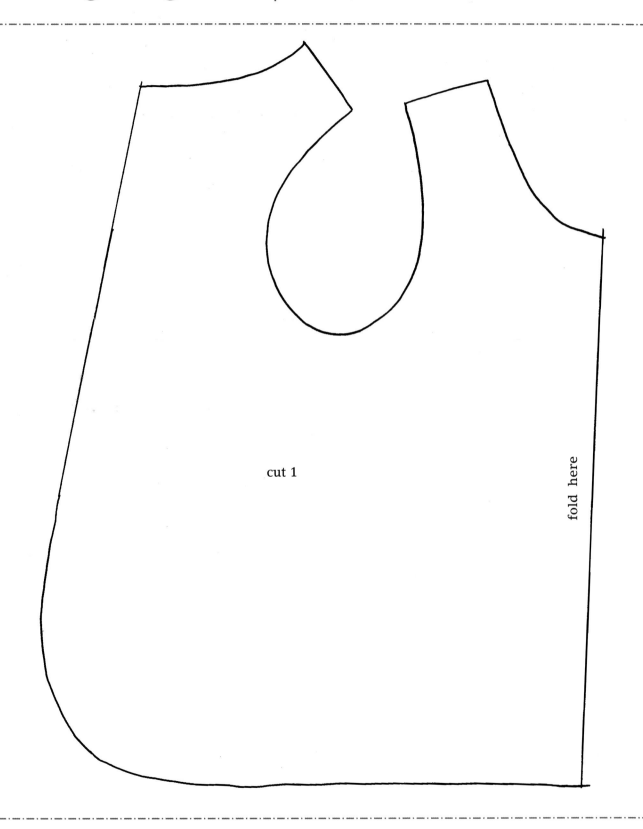

cut 1

fold here

Acknowledgments

Handmade is where it's at. It has real heart and soul, and craft bloggers are at the forefront of this movement. Mining sites and images all over the world, craft bloggers can spread information and enthusiasm with incredible force and speed, and they are the pulse of the new DIY movement. I would never have written this book had it not been for the amazing time I have spent getting to know other craft bloggers and maintaining my own craft blog. For everyone out there reading and contributing, I thank you for being a part of this amazing movement.

A big shout-out to:
The amazing talents at Potter Craft: Amy Sly, Lauren Monchik, Christina Schoen, and my editor, Shawna Mullen. I still get giddy when I look at these photos—thank you Alexandra Grablewski and Leslie Siebel for your amazing efforts.

Huge thanks to:
The invaluable words of wisdom from Sara Perry and Kay Gardiner; Mariko Fujinaka and my mother, Gayle Karol—for their time and diligence in providing copyediting help; Sarah Neuburger, Hillary Lang, Amanda Soule, and Alicia Paulson for their endless enthusiasm, inspiration, friendship, feedback, and just plain existence on this planet; Erin Salimena, my crazy-talented crafting partner in crime; my brother, Adam, for being my champion and supporter and for being so proud of me; my entire extended family for all their excitement; and my amazing husband, Pete, and my daughters, Sadie and Delia, who helped me write this book and *really* like all the stuff I make.

I believe (although she will deny it) that my agent, Sarah Sockit, is a superhero.

Resources

ABOUT THE FABRICS

This information will help you track down the fabrics featured in this book should you happen to fall in love with any of them. Please keep in mind that fabrics often get retired. This happens all the time and can be a real heartache. Try to stay flexible and you are sure to find something equally lovely if your favorite is sold out. Also, remember that even if a pattern is no longer being produced, it doesn't mean a local fabric shop (or online shop) has sold out yet. I called every fabric shop in Oregon to find the fabric I had my heart set on for my first daughter's nursery, and eventually I found it.

Café Curtains (page 98): "Flower Power," from Robert Kaufman. www.robertkaufman.com

Cat Tuffet in a Basket (page 74): "Vienna Stylized Flowers," from Alexander Henry. www.ahfabrics.com

Simple Bib (page 112) and Swing Swing Smock (page 126): "Johnny & Buck," from Moda. www.modafabrics.com

Pleated Beauty Handbag (page 68): "Arbor," by Kaffe Fasset from Rowan. www.knitrowan.com

Scalloped Baby Blanket (page 114): "Girlfriends" collection by Jennifer Paganelli from FreeSpirit. www.freespiritfabric.com

Clever Coasters (page 77): "Dottie Junior," collection from Moda. www.modafabrics.com

Pillows Three Ways, Ball Fringe Pillow, (page 89): "Storybook Garden," collection from Marcus Brothers. www.marcusbrothers.com

Easy Lap Quilt (page 86): "Vintage Flower Garden II," collection from Maywood Studios. www.maywoodstudio.com

VINTAGE FABRICS

Many of the projects in this book are made from vintage fabrics from my personal collection. There are loads of vintage fabrics out there just waiting to be made into great projects. Garage sales, thrift shops, and flea markets are great places to find vintage linens, napkins, and sometimes even uncut yardage, so keep your eyes open. There are online options for vintage fabrics as well:

eBay: www.ebay.com

Sharon's Vintage Fabrics: www.rickrack.com

Revived Fabrics www.revivalfabrics.com

NEW FABRICS

Developing a relationship with your local fabric shop is a must. Both chain stores and independently owned shops can give you that tactile experience that is so important when selecting fabrics. And thanks to the Internet, there are many online fabrics shops as well, perfect for shopping late at night in your pajamas.

Cia's Palette: www.ciaspalette.com

Reprodepot Fabric: www.reprodepotfabrics.com

Hancock's of Paducah: www.hancocks-paducah.com

e-Quilter: www.equilter.com

SewZanne's Fabrics www.sewzannesfabrics.com

Superbuzzy http://superbuzzy.com

Purl www.purlsoho.com/purl

The Fat Quarter Shop www.fatquartershop.com

Glorious Color www.gloriouscolor.com

Other Supplies

Fabric markers, paint dyes, and all of types of wonderful goodies:

Dharma Trading Company: www.dharmatrading.com/dyes.html

The Twining Thread www.twiningthread.com

M&J Trimming www.mjtrim.com

Sewing Notions and Supplies

Nancy's Notions: www.nancysnotions.com

Index